Divine Appointments

The Lighthouse by the Road

Bonnie S. Grau

TO THE GLORY OF GOD

TABLE OF CONTENTS

INTRODUCTION

We had just moved to York, Pennsylvania. The voice on the phone was friendly, but unfamiliar.

"My name is Joyce Ilgenfritz. Your daughter told me you had moved to York and we're having a home fellowship meeting at our house on Sunday night. I wanted to invite you to come."

Those words were like "apples of gold" (Proverbs 25:11) to someone who had just left her home of 36 years. I accepted Joyce's invitation and on that Sunday night my husband and I found our way to The Lighthouse, (the name by which the Ilgenfritz's home is known).

The evening changed my life. I left carrying a copy of *I Was a Stranger and . . .*, the first book about this remarkable couple and their ministry. Reading it took precedence over the boxes waiting to be unpacked.

Joyce and I didn't become friends immediately,

but when we did she told me people were inquiring about a second book and asked if I would write it. It was a step of faith – something with which she's quite familiar – because we still didn't know each other well and she knew little about my writing ability.

I don't remember exactly how I answered her, but I do know that we both became comfortable with the position that we would know *if* God wanted the book to be written and *when*.

On more than one occasion, when we thought it was time to begin the writing process, Joyce's attention was turned to something, or someone, else. We always accepted that as God's "wait."

Finally, in an unusual way, the Lord provided a quiet place for Joyce and me to begin working on the book. This volume is the result of waiting, watching and praying. It is only a small part of the story.

Bonnie Grau

CHAPTER ONE

BEGINNINGS

W hen Joyce and Morgan Ilgenfritz stood to their feet during a missionary meeting in the early 1970s, they both knew they were saying "yes" to God. On their way home that evening, Joyce told Morgan she thought they'd probably go to a far-off land—maybe to become house parents to missionaries' children. Morgan replied with his usual reserve and wisdom.

"It's not up to us to say what we'll do," he said. "We don't know what God has in mind. Let's just trust Him to show us what it is."

Joyce and Morgan didn't move to a far-off land, but they did become house parents—to the more than 375 people from all parts of the world who have lived at The Lighthouse. That number doesn't reflect the many who have shared a meal at the big dining room table, or others who have enjoyed a cup of coffee in front of the fireplace or in one of the flower gardens. After more than thirty years people continue to come. Some receive material assistance; all find a listening ear and praying hearts. Whatever their situations when they arrive, they are different when they leave.

Joyce and Morgan never aspired to live in a large house on a prominent street in their community. In fact, they were quite happy in their comfortable Cape Cod home on the outskirts of York, Pennsylvania. But shortly after they said yes to God, Claude Banks invaded their lives. Claude, the cantankerous old man whom no one wanted to be around, lived on Country Club Road. He had health problems and addictions which he frequently indulged.

Joyce, who is a nurse, had cared for Claude at various junctures. She often stopped in just to check on him. Then she and Morgan began getting calls from telephone operators (prompted by calls from Claude) during the night. After one such call, they went to Claude's house and took him, in a drunken state, to theirs. That's when his doctor issued an ultimatum—stay with them or move to a nursing home. Claude refused to consider the latter and looked to Joyce and Morgan. How could they say no when Claude needed them? More importantly, Claude needed the Lord and they knew that living with them could lead to his salvation. They agreed to take him in.

Claude stayed with the couple and their young children, Shonna, Mark and Amy, for more than a year before announcing that he wanted to find some-one to move into his house to take care of him and the property. Joyce told him she thought that was a wonderful idea and secretly began to anticipate life without Claude. However, Claude then revealed that she and Morgan were the persons he had in mind.

"Oh, that would never work," Joyce cried, thinking about (soon to be) four children in Claude's beautiful home.

"The kids can write on the walls if they want," Claude stated, "as long as you'll live there and take care of me."

Then Claude made a proposal whereby they could purchase his property.

Joyce and Morgan took the matter to God and began to sense this was His plan. Out of obedience to Him, they sold their house and entered into the agreement to take possession of Claude's. The transition was not easy, nor was the responsibility. Once they moved in, Claude became more demanding, and when his demands weren't met he was belligerent and verbally abusive. He'd take his frustrations out on Joyce, and then tell Morgan he was afraid she was having a nervous breakdown.

"I often felt trapped," Joyce admits. "Many times when everyone was asleep, I'd close the door to the basement, sit on the steps, and cry out to God."

Meanwhile, Claude's physical condition was deteriorating. One day the doctor said he probably wouldn't live through the night. Joyce shared the news with the children and later found Amy on the floor of her bedroom crying and praying.

"Please don't let Uncle Claude die, because he doesn't know You," the child was pleading. Joyce fell down beside her and together they prayed for Claude's salvation.

Claude didn't die that night. The next morning, he called Joyce to his bedside.

"I'm so sick," he said.

"I know you are," Joyce replied. "You almost died last night and if you had, we'd have never seen each other again. I know you said I shouldn't mention Jesus, but…"

"I'm ready," Claude responded.

Claude lived four days after receiving Christ and couldn't get enough of God's Word. In those four days, Joyce, her mother and her sister read him all four Gospels.

There's a plaque on the door of the room that belonged to Claude at The Lighthouse. A picture of Christ knocking on a door hangs nearby. Joyce bought the picture with a small gift of money Claude once gave her and used it to explain salvation to him. On the back of the picture are the names of all who have invited Christ into their lives at The Lighthouse. A few of the names are underlined. Joyce explains that those people are in heaven, and her eyes still fill with tears when she talks about how God answered their prayers for Uncle Claude.

CHAPTER TWO

MORGAN

J oyce was talking to a group of ladies who had just met her for the first time. Soon, someone asked about her husband.

Undaunted by the tears that filled her eyes, she answered, "When I think of Morgan, I think of Jesus."

By his own admission, Morgan did not remind anyone of Jesus for many years of his life.

"My parents loved me, but they worked all the time," he says. "I was my own boss. I got up, ate breakfast, and did what I wanted."

"My grandmother had me till I was three," he continued. "Then the Lord took her. She loved God's Word. I know she held me and prayed for me. Once when I was reading Psalm 91, I had the feeling she must have prayed those words over me."

After his grandmother's death, Morgan stayed with an aunt until he started to school. Then he went to a neighbor's house before and after school each day.

Morgan missed the presence of his mother during his early years. He remembers that there were thirteen kids on his street, and the other mothers often made cookies for after-school snacks.

"I was always included," he recalls, "but the kids never came to my house."

His father could be found at his workbench when he was at home. Today, Morgan can often be found at his.

"To me that's relaxation," he says.

Morgan did not put forth a lot of effort in school. He remembers one of his teachers telling him he'd never amount to anything. When he was sixteen, he decided he'd like to quit school and join the Navy. He convinced his mother to write a note saying he had her permission. He took the note to Miss Angler, another of his teachers, telling her what he planned to do.

Miss Angler told him he had to take the note to the principal. Following him down the hall, she asked to see the note. Without Morgan's knowledge, she tore it into shreds.

"What do we have here?" the principal asked as the two entered his office.

"This young man wants to quit school, but I think he has too much to offer," Miss Angler responded.

"Does he have a permission slip?" the principal inquired, holding out his hand.

Morgan couldn't believe his eyes when Miss

Angler dropped the shredded note into it.

Staring at the pieces of paper, the principal said, "I can't make head or tail of this," and dismissed them.

As they were returning to the classroom, Miss Angler said, "I saw you made your mother a pair of bookends the other week. Could you make me a pair, too?"

Not only did he make the bookends, he took on the responsibility of cutting Miss Angler's grass the following summer.

"She changed my life," Morgan says, tears filling his eyes.

"Today, I see myself in young boys who lack direction," he adds. "I never want to forget I was a young person. I had a lot of (influential) people in my life and I always hold them before me."

Probably for this reason, Morgan spent many years as a scoutmaster and mentoring young men has been his favorite role in The Lighthouse ministry.

Morgan did eventually graduate from high school and join the Navy. He bought Miss Angler a present in Cuba. When he returned with it, she invited him to speak to her class, giving him instructions to tell the students never to quit school.

"Thanks to Miss Angler, I didn't make a fatal mistake," Morgan declares.

On one of Morgan's furloughs from the Navy, his aunt suggested he visit the old homestead from which his family had moved when he was eight. She knew that Joyce's parents had purchased the house and lived there with Joyce and her eight brothers and sisters. Morgan took his aunt's advice and, although he remembered the Miller kids from years before, Joyce now caught his eye in a new way. He asked if she would write to him and soon they were seeing each other every time he came home. After a tour of duty in Korea he proposed and before long this only child became a beloved part of Joyce's large family.

Morgan spent most of his working years with Metropolitan Edison Electric Company. One of his jobs was to bring light to homes that were in darkness. It can be said that this is what he has done for many individuals through the years. He has been honored as Father of the Year by his church and as Outstanding Employee of the Year by Met Ed, and he and Joyce received the coveted Jefferson Award from a local television station for outstanding community service.

The light that never goes out in the lighthouse in Joyce and Morgan's front yard symbolizes the Light that came into Morgan's life when he spent weeks in the hospital fighting an eye infection many years ago. As he waited to know if he was going to have any sight at all, he was greatly influenced by his hospital roommate, John Hash.

"John and Morgan both had patches on their eyes, so they couldn't see each other," Joyce recalls. "Their beds were side by side and John would say, 'Brother, give me your hand.' And then he would pray."

"He prayed like Jesus was in the room," she

continues. "We were church-goers; you might say we were religious. But neither of us had ever heard anyone pray like John prayed. When I was worried about Morgan and our three children who were staying with friends and relatives, John prayed, 'Lord, here's this young couple with three children. You take care of those children and, Lord, please heal Morgan's eyes.'"

Morgan admits to being disappointed when he learned that he would lose the sight in his right eye, but today he says, "I look out of my left eye; Jesus looks out of the right one."

Many years after Morgan left that hospital, a man showed up on his doorstep asking for him. It was John Hash. The two "brothers" had a wonderful reunion.

CHAPTER THREE

FAMILY

Shonna, Mark, Amy and Beth—Joyce and Morgan's most precious jewels—different personalities, callings, and spiritual gifts. Through Mark, Miriam entered the family; through Amy, Steve, and through Beth, Jonas. Add to their number twenty grandchildren and there's always a birthday to celebrate.

Although Shonna, Mark, and Amy were born before Joyce and Morgan committed their lives to Christ, they were wanted and loved. They were also born before Claude became part of the family but came to love him as one of their own.

Beth was born after they moved into Claude's house. Because she was home during the day while her brother and sisters were in school, she enjoyed a special relationship with him.

"As she got older," Joyce says, "she helped me take care of Claude."

Beth often sat under the big dining room table while Joyce taught women's Bible studies at The Lighthouse. One day she asked her mother, "Is that lady who always wears the same shoes coming today?"

During that time, The Lighthouse served as the birthing center for pregnant women from New Life for Girls, a Christian drug rehabilitation center. When their delivery dates approached, the expectant mothers arrived and Joyce took them to the hospital and coached them through labor and delivery. When they were discharged, she brought them home and helped them establish a routine for their babies. A few weeks later, mothers and babies returned to New Life. A total of seventeen mothers and eighteen babies used these services (one mother had twins). Once, bassinets filled the living room with the five babies born to four mothers within a short time. Beth enjoyed being with the mothers and babies.

Amy invited Jesus into her heart the year Beth was born.

"I always say Amy and I grew up together in the Lord," Joyce says. "I accepted Christ when I was thirty-two, and six months later Amy came to Him. From the beginning she had a great love for God's Word and we often read it together."

One morning when Joyce was packing Amy and Mark's lunches for school, she turned to them and said, "You know, Amy and Mark, somewhere in this world God has a person for you to spend your life with. I think we should pray about that right now."

"O Mother..." Mark said, as Joyce took their hands and interrupted him with her prayer.

Amy and Mark both felt called of God to be missionaries. After completing his schooling at Christian School of York, Mark went to LeTourneau College in Plainview, Texas and then transferred to Prairie Bible College in Alberta, Canada. When Amy enrolled at St. Paul Bible College in Minnesota, he called his parents.

"Mother and Dad," he said, "I want to transfer to St. Paul. I can't see Amy being so far from home without someone to look after her."

So, Mark and Amy were both at St. Paul Bible College. Miriam Ewart and Steve Nehlsen were also there —Miriam from Lincoln, Nebraska, by way of Zaire, Central Africa, and Steve from Burkina Faso, West Africa. Both were MKs (missionary kids). God heard and answered Joyce's prayer, prayed years earlier in The Lighthouse kitchen, and brought Mark and Amy's life partners from "somewhere in this world."

Shonna

Being the oldest, Shonna had left home to attend Nyack and King's Colleges in New York before The Lighthouse ministry began. During her career with Pennsylvania Power and Light, she advanced to the rank of major in the Army Reserves and was deployed during both Desert Storm and the war in Iraq.

It was through Shonna's involvement with fundraisers for New Life for Girls that Joyce and Morgan became involved in the New Life ministry.

God also used Shonna to save The Lighthouse.

Occasionally, when Morgan "did the books," he'd tell Joyce they needed to think about selling the house. Finally, he decided the time had come. Joyce wasn't convinced it was the thing to do, but she believed if it wasn't, God would stop it. Together, she and Morgan looked at condominiums and went so far as to pick flooring for one.

A young couple from their church expressed interest in purchasing the property for a ministry to York College students. When they found a financial backer, a time was set to formalize the agreement. On the morning of the impending meeting, Shonna called and said she was coming over to talk.

"Mother and Dad," she said when she arrived. "I couldn't sleep last night. I don't want you to sell. I want you to keep doing what you're doing. I'll pick up the mortgage payments. If the day comes that this place is too much to take care of, I'll see that you get help."

"What's going to happen when Amy and Steve come home from Africa," she continued, "and when Mark and Miriam come with all their children? A condominium isn't going to hold everyone."

God had stopped the sale. Joyce placed a call to the potential buyers and the ministry continued uninterrupted.

Mark and Miriam

Shortly after Mark met Miriam, he decided she was the woman he wanted to marry. The first time he visited her home, he asked for and received her parents' permission. Then he called his parents. When Joyce expressed surprise, Mark reminded her that she had prayed for ten years and told her that Miriam's mother had done the same. He said that he and Miriam were sure this was God's will.

Although Mark and Miriam shared a desire for a large family, they began to feel overwhelmed while expecting their fifth child. Shortly before the baby's birth, God dealt with them and they decided to step out in faith and allow Him to provide for whatever number of children He gave them. They have fifteen children. Mark is a self-employed electrician. His second oldest son has apprenticed and works with him in the trade.

Joyce recalls a conversation with Mark after the eighth child was born.

"Now you have eight," she said. "That's a wonderful family."

"Mother, Amy and I both graduated from Bible college," Mark replied. "God called Amy to the mission field. He called Miriam and me to have children. It's very important to us that we have the backing of our parents."

"From that day on, Morgan and I decided they have our support 100 percent," Joyce says. "This is between them and the Lord."

When Mark and Morgan once discussed the size of Mark's family, Mark told his dad how he and

Miriam had agreed to allow the Lord to give them as many children as He planned for them.

"If He has a plan for them," Mark said, "He will supply all their needs."

"As long as I know you're being good parents, you have my support," Morgan told him.

"They have a system that works," Joyce says. "The Lord had to show me I'm just the grandma. We do all we can and we pray faithfully. They're doing a great job. They emphasize what's really important and take time to do things I never would have."

Mark and Miriam both believe in family devotions and end the day with them as often as possible.

"Although every night is our goal, every night doesn't happen," Mark says honestly. During devotions, Mark teaches a Bible lesson, they sing, share prayer requests and pray. Amy and Steve are high on their request list and depend on their prayers.

Whenever they can arrange it, Morgan and Joyce enjoy being there for that time.

"You should hear those children pray," Joyce says.

She smiles when she remembers how ten-year-old David once prayed that everyone in the room would accept Jesus as Lord and Savior. To her knowledge, only the youngest hadn't yet made that decision and she wasn't old enough to understand it.

Once, when Morgan's mother (then ninety-three) was with them, one of the children prayed, "Oh, Lord, help us all to live to be old."

All the children have Bible names and each knows the story of his name. Reading takes the place of television in the home, and the children often sit around the big kitchen table discussing what they've read.

Music is another common denominator. Ten of the children play instruments including dulcimer, Uillean pipes (a type of bagpipe and tin whistle), Bodhran (an Irish drum), mandolin, highland pipes, guitar, alto recorder, flute, banjo, violin, piano, and organ. Miriam plays the flute and piccolo. One of the boys played piano for the school choir in his senior year and another accompanied the choir on the organ the next year.

"They work and play together," Joyce says. "When there's work to be done, they all do it—whether it's picking beans or making apple cider or sauerkraut."

Amy and Steve

Amy and Steve are in their fourteenth year of missionary service. Their first daughter, Abigail Joy, was seven weeks old when they left for language school in Paris. They were expecting their second child when they left Paris for Côte d'Ivoire. Shortly after they arrived in Côte d'Ivoire, a boy was born prematurely, miles from proper medical care. Samuel lived only eight hours and is buried in African soil. Morgan has lovingly crafted a memorial for him in a flower bed at The Lighthouse.

Because of Samuel's death, Joyce wanted to be with Amy for her next baby's birth. Not only did she travel to Africa when Kari was born, but again eight years later to help bring Peter into the world.

After twelve years in Côte d'Ivoire, political unrest and Amy's abduction (chapter 20) forced Amy and Steve to move to Burkina Faso.

Steve's parents served faithfully in Burkina for thirty-six years. Not long after they retired, his dad died suddenly. So, to be back in the place where he spent the first fifteen years of his life has special meaning for Steve.

Soon after he went to Burkina, Steve visited a national church and was asked to introduce himself. When he said he was Steve Nehlsen, the son of Jesse and Herb Nehlsen, the pastor's eyes filled with tears.

"You are standing under your father's tree," he said, meaning that Steve's dad had helped him put down the roots of his ministry there.

Losing a child, abduction, a forced furlough, having to leave the people they'd worked with for twelve years... Africa was hard. But, it was also where Amy and Steve's hearts were. When they lived in York between assignments, Peter drew pictures for their night guard "at home" in Côte d'Ivoire. Africa is home.

Beth and Jonas

Although she was the only one born after her mother became a Christian, Beth perhaps struggled more than the others throughout her decision-making years. Frequently she wavered between good and bad choices, sometimes choosing the latter.

"We prayed for Beth a lot during that time, reminding God that she was His child," Joyce recalls.

Beth went to cosmetology school from high

school, and enjoyed both the training and a subsequent job. An allergy to the chemicals, however, cut that career short. She enrolled at Eastern Mennonite College in Harrisonburg, Virginia but told her dad after the first semester that it was a waste of his money because she didn't know what she wanted to do. She eventually attended York Business Institute and acquired an Associate Degree in Business Management. Following her marriage to Jonas, she took classes at Toccoa Falls College in Georgia, and after their daughters Amee and Ashley were in school, she completed a Bachelor of Science Degree in Christian Ministry Leadership. She has served as children's director in their church.

As part of her degree work, Beth wrote a paper about her mother entitled *Lessons for a Lifetime*. In the introduction she says, "I have had the privilege of walking in her shadow, as she has followed the path that God had for her and my father. She has taught by example and has sincerely lived up to the first three letters of her name—joy!"

Then, using all the letters of Joyce's name, she listed these five lessons:

1) Jesus is the Answer
2) Other People Matter
3) Yield to God's Will
4) Call Out to Jesus
5) Exemplified Unconditional Love

As Beth and Jonas (one of The Lighthouse miracles whose story is told in the next chapter) minister together, rear their children to honor God, and open their home to strangers who have lost their way, they are living examples of the lessons they both learned at The Lighthouse.

Grandchildren

"I have to laugh at people's reactions when they find out that we have so many grandchildren," Joyce says. "They usually ask two questions, 'Do you know all their names and do you remember their birthdays?' How could I forget either one?"

She names Mark's children: Seth, Benjamin, Josiah, Hannah, Naomi, Noah, Esther, David, Elijah, Jedidiah, Ephraim, Moriah, Hosannah, Jerusha and Emmanuel.

"Some day they will all be beacons for Jesus, letting their light shine for Him," she states. "It is so neat to see how God is at work in each of their lives. All the older children have ideas of what they want to be when they grow up: Seth, a doctor; Ben, an electrician like his father; Josiah, a missionary bush pilot; Hannah, a nurse; Naomi, an artist and teacher; Noah, an astronaut; Esther, a mother with a lot of children; David, a missionary; Elijah, a farmer and hunter; Jedidiah, a scientist; Ephraim, a builder; Moriah, an archeologist; Hosannah, a nurse. I'm anxious to hear what Jerusha and Emmanuel will want to be," she says.

"Some of the children change their ideas as time passes," Miriam comments, "but Seth definitely feels called to be a doctor, Benjamin an electrician, and Naomi an artist and possibly a teacher. Noah's had a desire to be an astronaut for years, and Esther, a mother. We'll just have to see where they all end up."

Miriam takes delight in a verse in Proverbs 14 which says *"Where no oxen are, the manger is clean (NASB)."*

"Our manger is not always clean," she says, "but 100 years from now that won't matter. What will matter is what we and our children have done for the Lord."

Joyce enjoys watching Mark's family do many of the things her family did as she was growing up. "I get flashbacks to my childhood," she says.

"But," she adds, "it is amazing to see how Morgan has adjusted to our son having fifteen children when he was an only child. He is a super grandpa and the children dearly love him. Once when we were driving home he said, 'I can't believe our one son has ten sons and five daughters. Isn't God good?'"

Both Morgan and Joyce admit that being grand-parents to twenty grandchildren, with two of them in Colorado and three in Africa, takes creativity—especially considering the complexities of The Lighthouse. Joyce searches throughout the year for gifts and cards, and never waits until an occasion arrives to prepare for it. Morgan has the responsibility of mailing packages to faraway places; together they make an effort to be on hand for all Mark's family's birthday celebrations. If it's not possible to be there on the actual day, they go when they can and sometimes have to celebrate more than one birthday at a time.

Recently, Joyce was in a store right after Valentine's Day and saw a little picture frame and two heart boxes.

"I didn't buy them," she says, "but that night I had a conversation with the Lord."

"Lord, I have all these grandchildren," I said. "How can I stay connected with them?"

"I went to sleep," she continues, "and later awoke to hear the Lord saying, 'Go back to that store and get the frame and the two boxes.' Then He explained what I was to do with them."

Joyce put the frame on her kitchen windowsill and the boxes on the counter. She found a picture of each grandchild and put each one's name on a piece of paper. She put the papers in one of the boxes. Each week, she draws a name from the box, puts that child's picture in the frame and places the name in the other box for the next time around.

Then she calls the child to report that he (or she) is her "Star of the Week," and asks if there's anything special she can pray about. The child knows he'll hear from her again by way of another phone call, a note or a package—or possibly all three.

Miriam tells about five-year-old Moriah getting off the phone and announcing proudly, "I'm Grandma's Star of the Week."

When six-year-old Ashley (in Colorado) got her call, she told her grandma that there was a girl in her class who was saying mean things about her.

"You just be nice to her and I'll be praying," Joyce responded.

In the next call, Ashley said, "That little girl has been so nice to me and I know it's because you've been praying."

Later, Ashley wrote this story in school about being "Star of the Week."

I am my grandma's star of her week. She pulled the name out of a hat and she drew me. She only put all the cousins in the hat. Two of the cousins are spending tonight (with Grandma). They picked me. Grandma called me. She is sending me a present in the mail. I am so happy I am her star of the week.

"Aunt" Sue

Susan Newcomer, Shonna's long-time friend and confidant, is "like an adopted daughter" to Joyce and Morgan. "Aunt Sue" to the children, she remembers each one generously and lovingly. She's part of holiday celebrations and vacations and is always willing to lend a helping hand when there's a need.

Dwayne

Once a delinquent youth, Dwayne Woodring came to The Lighthouse at the age of sixteen as a foster son. He had been expelled from high school for fighting and was working as a dishwasher at York Hospital. Morgan's compassionate heart and firm hand were instrumental in turning Dwayne's life around. When he finally accepted Christ as his Savior, he began to change on the inside. Today, he is happily married and the father of three children. He and his family can also be found at Lighthouse gatherings.

Others

Joyce recalls many more who could be included in a "family" chapter.

"Some who have lived here have moved on with their lives and we may hear from them occasionally. Others remain part of The Lighthouse family," she says. "I'm looking forward to a big reunion in heaven. That's probably the only time we'll have one."

Visits, letters, phone calls, and e-mails help this large family to stay in touch. But the common thread that binds them together is prayer. From Pennsylvania, Colorado, Africa, and many places in between, prayer unites all their hearts under the umbrella of God's love.

CHAPTER FOUR

JONAS

Beth was working in a beauty salon at a mall a half-hour from home.

"Mother," she said one day, "I want you to meet this neat guy. His name is Jonas and he works at a store across the mall. If you and Amy come in someday, I'll have him come over."

A week later, Joyce and Amy went to Beth's workplace. Beth called Jonas and he came to the salon.

"I was shocked," Joyce remembers. "He had long hair, an earring, and baggy jeans. I wasn't ready for what I saw."

"But," she hastened to add, "he was very friendly."

After Jonas left, Joyce addressed her concerns.

"Beth, I just don't know what you see in him," she said.

Without hesitation, Beth replied, "Mom, he's got a lot of potential."

A couple days later, Beth approached Joyce.

"We have to pray for Jonas," she said. "He's very close to his mother and she's very sick."

Later, Beth told Joyce that when Jonas learned she and her parents were praying for his mother, it "blew him away." Eventually, Jonas' mother recovered from her illness.

After a while, Beth gave Jonas a copy of the book that had been written about her family and he read it in one day.

"I want to meet your dad, too," he said when he returned the book.

When Joyce heard this, she told Beth to invite him for dinner.

Beth issued the invitation but asked if she could cut his hair first.

Jonas offered no resistance and Beth gave him not one, but two, haircuts.

Then Jonas asked, "Should I take out my earring?"

Beth replied, "It probably wouldn't hurt, but you do what you think."

"It means more to me to meet your dad," Jonas replied, "than to wear this earring."

When Jonas arrived at The Lighthouse— short hair and no earring—and Beth introduced him to Morgan, Jonas stuck out his hand and said, "How do you like my haircut?"

"Jonas talked all through dinner," Joyce recalled. "My heart just went out to him."

When he was ready to leave, she said, "Jonas,

the next time you come, I have something I want to give you."

"Okay, but what is it?" Jonas asked eagerly.

"Don't worry. The next time you are here, I will give it to you," Joyce replied.

"I felt I needed a week to pray," she explained later. "I just knew he was going to be my son-in-law."

A week later, Jonas came back. Before dinner, he asked, "What was that gift you had for me?"

Joyce led Jonas and Beth to the back porch and picked up a copy of a booklet entitled *Four Spiritual Laws*. Then she began to tell Jonas that God had a wonderful plan for his life.

Paging through the booklet to illustrations of the natural man and the spiritual man, she said, "Jonas, which man are you?"

"Oh, that's my life," he said, pointing to the drawing depicting chaos (the natural man).

"Which man do you want to be?" she asked.

"That one," he answered, pointing to the symbols of order (the spiritual man).

By the end of the booklet, Jonas knew what he had to do. He prayed and accepted Jesus as his Savior and Beth rededicated her life to the Lord.

Later that night when she was alone, Joyce wrote in her journal, "Today Jonas Wharton received Christ. I know that someday he will be my son-in-law."

A short while later, Beth again asked her mother to pray for Jonas.

She explained that his roommate drank and did

drugs and that Jonas was having a rough time resisting the temptation to join him.

Joyce shared Beth's request with Morgan. Then she said, "Honey, I've been thinking about something."

"Now what?" Morgan asked.

"I think Jonas should come here to live."

"Do you really think that's a good idea?" Morgan asked.

"Honey, Jonas is our responsibility. He's never had a good father figure."

"How can we get in touch with him?" Morgan inquired.

"I know," Joyce replied, "our telephone bill. I'm sure Beth has called him."

Joyce found the bill, called the number, and Beth answered the phone.

When she told her about their conversation, Beth asked, "Where would he live?"

Joyce knew what she was thinking. Beth had just redecorated and moved into the basement bedroom because there were five other girls living upstairs.

"Beth," she said. "What's more important to you—Jonas or the bedroom you just did over?"

After a moment's thought, Beth said she'd move back upstairs and Jonas could have her room.

The next day, Jonas pulled in the driveway with all his earthly belongings in his Chevette. When he was settled, Joyce called Beth and him into the living room.

Seating them on the sofa, she said, "I don't want

any hanky-panky going on in this house. I can't be here all the time, but the Lord is."

Several months after Jonas moved in, he asked Morgan for Beth's hand and in less than a year they were married.

Jonas had a hard time deciding what he wanted to do the first year of their marriage and changed jobs several times. Beth was disillusioned and started to wonder if she had made a mistake. Then Jonas took a discipleship course and began to grow in his faith. Soon, he announced he felt God wanted him to go to Bible school. He enrolled at Toccoa Falls College in Georgia and Beth worked at the college while attending classes.

While pursuing his studies, Jonas became the youth pastor at a nearby church. Following graduation, he and Beth served there for several years. Then he was asked to candidate for a similar position in Aurora, Colorado. He was hired and served as pastor of students and families for four years. When the senior pastor of the church resigned, Jonas was chosen to take his place.

Joyce went to Colorado for Mother's Day soon after he became senior pastor. She sat near the front of the church that Sunday morning and watched him begin the service. Then she heard him say, "I want you to meet a very special mother, my mother-in-love. She is the person who introduced me to the Lord."

Through tears, Joyce looked at the young man

standing behind the pulpit.

It was as if she could hear Beth saying, "But Mom, he's got a lot of potential."

CHAPTER FIVE

MORGAN ON MISSION

The year was 1989. The pastor of Morgan and Joyce's church asked a visiting missionary from Burkina Faso if there was anything specific the church could be praying about. Without hesitation the missionary replied, "Pray for the Senofou, an unreached people group."

The missionary returned to his field in Africa and the church began to pray. Soon word came back that there had been evangelistic services in the town of Banfora. A Senofou man had accepted Jesus, was disowned by his family, and had gone to the town of Douna looking for a church. There was no church in Douna.

David Shady, the missionary who had visited the York church, heard of the situation and began to investigate the possibility of building a church in Douna. He contacted Jim Grant, pastor of the praying church in York, and an idea was born.

Pastor Grant shared with his congregation the amount of money that would be needed to build a church in Douna. In six weeks, the money came in. Then David Shady wrote that it would be a good idea to send a work team to help with the building. Pastor Grant shared that the following Sunday.

"I knew right away I was to go," Morgan recalled. "I didn't know how, but I knew I would."

Six other men knew, too, and soon a team was assembled. They worked through a myriad of details, including approval from their church headquarters, visas, and travel arrangements. A schedule was set up which allowed them a week to build the church and a week to visit other areas of Christian and Missionary Alliance ministry in Africa.

"The agreement was that the mud block walls would be up to the windowsills by the time we arrived (in Douna)," Morgan said. "We got there on a Sunday night and looked around. Finally, I asked, 'Where are we building?'"

"Right over there in that sweet potato patch," someone answered.

"I don't see any building over there," Morgan said.

"Well, there's a problem," was the reply. "We got the foundation poured, but we didn't get the walls up."

Since the church was to be completed for the following Sunday's service, the pressure was on.

Morgan smiles as he recalls one setback. There were three nationals laying blocks on one side of the building and three Americans laying blocks on the other. Looking across at the national's side, Morgan said, "There's something wrong here."

Upon closer examination, the Americans realized that the nationals had squared their blocks off before starting to lay them and the Americans were laying the blocks as they came from the ground. Therefore, one side was straight, the other was leaning. From that point on, two men were assigned to squaring blocks for the Americans and the work proceeded.

The team worked diligently all week. Only by beginning at 5:00 a.m. Saturday and working until after dark, using lights from trucks, did they complete the project. At 9:00 Sunday morning when they drove up to the building, African Christians were singing praises in their new church.

Was it worth it?

Morgan says that just seeing the faces of the people was worth it, but he also remembers a personal blessing.

"The Lord makes no mistakes," he said. "My daughter was preparing to go to Africa as a missionary. He allowed me to go first and see what she was going to experience."

"Amy won't have any trouble here at all," he relayed to Joyce in a phone call. "I was her trailblazer."

Then he recalled two other aspects of the trip.

"We always had prayer before we started to work," he said. "One out of the three nationals who were helping us was a believer; the daughter of another was seriously ill. The believer told us about her illness and we prayed for her. By the end of the week, she was on the road to recovery."

He related the second with a twinkle in his eyes.

"Every day the missionaries would bring sweet rolls and coffee to us. We'd stop working long enough to drink the coffee, eat the sweet rolls, wash the cups, and hand them to the Africans. I think we introduced the coffee break to the African workers."

The year was 1992. During the first trip, the team had stayed in the village of Sindou. Each evening they had prayer meetings. The last night they were there, the village chief came to the prayer meeting, accompanied by a Christian pharmacist. The pharmacist told the men that the chief wanted a church like the one in Douna in his town. Before they left, the men prayed, "Lord, if you want a church in Sindou, You make it happen."

Two-and-a-half years later, two teams of seven were preparing to build a cement block church in Sindou. Morgan was on the second team.

Amy and Steve were now in Bouake, the second largest city in Côte d'Ivoire, West Africa. Joyce and Morgan left a week before Morgan's team to visit them. At the end of the week, the two families traveled to Sindou and Steve helped with the building. The workers slept in tents which had been erected at the mission compound and the women and children stayed with the missionary's family. In the two weeks the two teams were there, they completed the church, put a new roof on the missionary's home and repaired their plumbing.

Was it worth it?

"It was most rewarding," Morgan replies. "Just seeing how grateful the people were to be able to gather under protection from the hot sun and hearing them worshiping in their language was worth it.

"When we walked in on Sunday morning, they were smiling from ear to ear. They had chairs up front for us and we sat as honored guests. Yes, it was worth it."

The year was 2000. A member of Morgan's church had a missionary friend in Haiti. The friend asked if some men could come to repair transformers at a hospital. Two years earlier an engineer had surveyed the situation, purchased materials, and sent them down. But nobody knew how to remove the old transformers and put the new ones up and there was no guarantee the material hadn't fallen to thievery. Soon, however, several people volunteered to go, but nobody had the know-how to do the job.

Morgan's phone rang.

"We need your expertise," the team leader said. "We have the workers, but we don't have any idea how to go about it."

"I didn't know the particulars," Morgan said. "If I had, I probably wouldn't have gone.

"But," he added, "it was my line of work and they had the manpower and hopefully the equipment."

Morgan prayed and agreed to go. Then he called the man who had purchased the material two years earlier. All he could get from the man was, "Good luck."

"When I retired (from the electric company) nine years earlier," Morgan said, "my boss asked if I could use a lot of electrical stuff they were getting rid of."

Never one to throw anything out, Morgan accepted it and stored it in his shed. He is convinced that the Lord provided that block and tackle, rope, and other materials for this project.

"When the Lord said He'd supply our needs," he continued, "He didn't say we'd need the stuff tomorrow. Nine years later, I took it to Haiti. And before I went, I had a chance at a GPU retiree's luncheon to thank some of the people who taught me my skills and tell them how those supplies would be used."

Claiming the verse *"I can do all things through Christ who strengthens me"* (Philippians 4:13), Morgan and the men worked on top of the hospital to replace the three transformers. Rather than the anticipated week, the job only took three days, so they rewired a switching station, put a new electrical system in the hospital and wired a maintenance building.

"The only thing that wasn't functioning when we left was the X-ray machine," Morgan recalled. "We learned later that they just had to switch a voltage lever and it also worked."

Today the field hospital continues to operate.

Was it worth it?

"Yes," Morgan says without reservation. "If you help a little or a lot, it's worth it!"

CHAPTER SIX

ALLELUIA

Once, at a missionary conference, a man put his hand on Joyce's shoulder and said, "I want to tell you something, Joyce. You have a missionary heart."

Joyce thought back to the night when she and Morgan had said yes to God.

"In my heart I wanted to be a foreign missionary so badly, but God had other plans," she said. "For us, the Great Commission meant opening our home to the world. Instead of sending us to a foreign country, he sent our daughter Amy. I'm so glad she heard the call and was willing to go.

"You can't imagine how hard I've tried to learn other languages," she added, laughing. "Foreign students who've lived here have attempted to teach me theirs, but I just can't seem to learn them. Yet in spite of this I've been to Africa three times, France twice, Japan, Korea, and the Philippines.

"When Amy and Steve were in language school in France, I went to visit them," she continued. "Before I left, I studied French, using tapes. When I got there, I spent seven hours in Charles de Gaulle Airport and couldn't even remember the word for bathroom."

Joyce's face brightened as she recalled more from that experience.

"Since smiling is universal I just sat and smiled," she said. "Many people smiled back, but there was one lady I really connected with. We tried communicating in sign language but weren't very successful. Then I remembered a word that is the same in every language."

"'Alleluia,' I said."

"Her eyes lit up and we both knew what we had in common."

"'Alleluia,' she answered, grinning from ear to ear."

"Much later," Joyce continued, "I was standing in a long customs line and looked across several other lines. There stood the lady."

"'Alleluia,' I mouthed."

"'Alleluia,' she answered."

Joyce still has a passion for international people. A large map in The Lighthouse kitchen marks locations all over the world from which houseguests have come. It is a focal point for prayer as Joyce and Morgan remember those who have been part of their family.

Recently when Amy and Steve were home from

Africa, Melba, a Christian from India, spent three months at The Lighthouse. One evening she cooked dinner for Joyce, Morgan, Amy, Steve and Myuki (a Japanese student). When they sat down to the table, Morgan prayed. Then Melba prayed in Hindi, Steve in Jula (an African dialect), Amy in French, and Myuki in Japanese.

"When it came around to me," Joyce said. "I just prayed 'Alleluia, alleluia, alleluia.' It was the language of my heart for another special moment."

CHAPTER SEVEN

OUR FAIR LADY

J oyce attended a one-room schoolhouse for her first eight years of school. Mr. Moul was her teacher all eight years. The annual York Fair was very important to Mr. Moul. His students collected leaves and berries to exhibit and often won ribbons.

School was always closed on Tuesday of Fair Week and the children were given free tickets to go to the fair.

"Since we had a large family, we didn't go many places," Joyce recalled. "But we did attend the fair. Mother would pack a big lunch, Dad would load up the station wagon and off we'd go."

Joyce remembers her mother taking her to see the midgets. She was always curious about them but saw them with different eyes after she became a Christian.

When Morgan and Joyce moved to The Light-house, Claude told them they should sign up to become members of the Fair Association. He explained that the association only took 250 members and it may take twenty-five years for their name to come up.

To make him happy, they agreed and listed Claude as one of their sponsors. Once the form was mailed, they forgot about it. Twenty-nine years later a letter arrived saying they were eligible to join the Fair Association.

Morgan wasn't very excited.

"Do you want to do it?" he asked.

"Honey, I don't care how much it costs, I do," Joyce replied.

Shonna overheard the conversation and said, "Dad, the way Mother loves the fair, you have to do it."

Morgan agreed. (He and Joyce both enter flowers in the fair exhibits and have won prizes for their dahlias and roses.)

Every year the association holds a special event day for members and their immediate families. Once, twenty-three members of Morgan and Joyce's family (including seventeen of their then-nineteen grandchildren) attended, breaking the all-time record for that event.

To Joyce, the fair is an opportunity. She passes the entrance on her way to work and begins to pray two weeks before opening day. Because her membership affords convenient parking and free entry, she's able to go to the fair many times during the week.

No fair worker is too insignificant for her interest.

She has been known to take ham and cheese sandwiches to the parking attendants and salads to the ladies who care for the restrooms. She also buys apples from one of the fruit stands to give to fair workers.

She still visits the midgets and tells them that if they know Jesus they'll have perfect bodies in heaven. She gives Bibles to exhibitors and has prayed with many about personal needs or to accept Jesus as Savior. She takes an interest in their families and has kept children of fair workers in her home.

When it was announced at a recent association meeting that members could purchase a tree in honor or memory of a loved one, Morgan acted quickly.

"I didn't have to think twice about it," he explained.

The flowering Japanese tree that he purchased for the family bears the inscription, *"In honor of Our Fair Lady, Joyce Ilgenfritz."*

Reflecting on it, Shonna said, "Mother went to the fair almost every day, even before the lifetime membership. She had fair stories as long as I can remember. Actually, getting the lifetime membership was like her just rewards."

CHAPTER EIGHT

FAIR FRIENDS

"The Smallest Man in the World."

"Let's go see him," Joyce said to Morgan.

"Here's fifty cents, you go," Morgan replied.

Joyce bought a ticket and followed an upward ramp to a fenced-in area. When she reached the top, she was shocked at what she saw. Instead of the tuxedo-clad figure pictured outside, there was an 18-inch-man dressed in a T-shirt, sitting on a skateboard. His head was normal size, his trunk badly deformed, his arms and legs dwarfed. She later learned he had no spinal cord.

The man's name was Pete. He was wearing a microphone around his neck. Pete looked up at Joyce, smiled and asked, "Do you have any questions?"

"Yes, I do," Joyce replied. "Do you know Jesus?"

"Yes, I do," Pete responded without hesitation.

"Oh, that is wonderful," Joyce exclaimed.

"Someday you'll have a perfectly formed body."

"I'm waiting for that day," Pete said.

The sign outside said that Pete had a five-foot-five-inch wife and two children. Joyce told Pete she'd like to meet his wife.

When Joyce went home that day, she made a sign that said, *"Man looks at the outward appearance, but the Lord looks at the heart"* (1 Samuel 16:7). Then she called a few friends and told them to visit Pete at the fair. She also called John Oldfield, a pastor- friend.

That evening, just as the fair was about to close, Joyce and Pastor John took the sign to the fairgrounds and positioned it beside Pete's skateboard. Then they knocked on the door of Pete's trailer behind the midway and introduced themselves to his wife. She invited them in and asked them to wait while she went to get Pete. In a few moments, they watched in amazement as he rolled into the middle of the room on his skateboard, propelled by a friendly push. His wife followed him into the room, picked him up, put him on a chair at the table and made coffee for everyone. They all chatted while enjoying the coffee, then gathered around Pete and prayed. Later that night, when Joyce and Pastor John tried to leave the fairgrounds, they discovered they were locked in. Fortunately, they were able to find someone who could let them out.

Joyce continued to visit Pete and his family throughout the week. His wife told her that she had first seen Pete at the grand opening of a shopping center and, as they were talking, the Lord told her she was going to marry him.

"No, God, no," she had cried in her heart. But she went back every day that week and eventually what God had told her happened. In time, they had the two children, a son who didn't inherit Pete's condition and a daughter who did.

As Joyce got to know Pete's wife throughout the week, she asked if there was anything she could do for her.

"Well, Friday night is such a busy night at the fair," she said. "I should help to sell tickets. Could you keep the children?"

When Friday came, Amy and Beth went with Joyce to the fairgrounds. They took the children home and the girls spent the evening entertaining them. It was a memorable occasion and a sad time when the two families finally had to say goodbye.

Steve

Steve was the snake handler at the fair one year. Joyce doesn't like snakes.

"I hate snakes," she confesses. "I really hate snakes."

But, as was her custom, she prayed before entering the fairgrounds and soon found herself standing outside the snake tent talking to a young girl with a snake wrapped around her neck. The girl said her name was Liz, and as Joyce observed her manner of dress and imagined her lifestyle, Joyce's heart went out to her.

She learned that Liz was a college student who had met Steve in a restaurant where she was working. He had persuaded her to accompany him, sell tickets and attract people to the snake display for the summer.

Joyce reached in her pocketbook and handed Liz a little Bible.

"My mother would be so happy," Liz said, accepting it. "I know she is praying for me."

"Well, Liz," Joyce said. "Life is a matter of choices. Please don't make wrong ones."

After Joyce had talked with Liz, she told her she'd like to meet the owner of the snakes.

"He's inside the tent," Liz said, selling her a ticket to go in.

"I can't believe I'm paying two dollars to look at snakes," Joyce thought.

"Are you Steve?" she asked the man who welcomed her. "I'm interested in your snakes." (Although she didn't like snakes, Joyce really was interested because she knew God wanted her to talk to Steve.) Soon Steve was proudly showing her the reptiles.

"This is an African snake," he said pointing to one.

"I have a daughter in Africa," Joyce replied, trying to redirect the conversation.

"This type of snake has killed thousands of people," Steve answered.

When Joyce went home that evening and told Morgan about her visit, he was shocked.

"You were in with the snakes?" he exclaimed. "I've got to see that."

The next time Joyce went to the fair, Morgan accompanied her and met Steve.

Joyce continued to visit Steve throughout the week, taking him ham sandwiches and apples. He always invited her into the tent and she never had to pay the entrance fee again. Each time she went, she shared a little more about the Lord and on one visit she gave Steve a Bible. One day she noticed that Liz wasn't outside the tent. When she inquired, Steve told her that Liz had gone home.

Later in the week, Steve pointed to one of the snakes.

"That snake's pregnant," he said.

"Oh, that's interesting," Joyce said. "How do snakes mate?"

Encouraged by her interest, Steve explained the process in detail.

"Incredible," Joyce said when he finished. "How can anyone doubt there's a God?"

On another visit, Steve told Joyce he had recently become very ill while driving his truck. He said his mother, who had been dead for years, appeared to him and told him to go to the hospital.

"I hate to tell you this, Steve," Joyce said, "but that wasn't your mother. That was the Holy Spirit. He directed you to the hospital."

Joyce missed the last day of the fair, but returned to the grounds the next morning to retrieve her containers and ribbons from the flowers she had exhibited. The fairgrounds were almost deserted, but she drove around to where Steve had been. He was still there, taking down his tent. He looked surprised to see her.

"Joyce," he said, a big smile on his face. "I prayed with a man from Child Evangelism Fellowship yesterday to receive Christ. I didn't think I'd get a chance to tell you."

Joyce was elated. As she and Steve rejoiced together, she thanked God for leading her to the snake tent and for other Christians who faithfully minister at the Fair each year.

Richard

Richard was the "Blooming Onion" man.

Joyce visited with him one year. Morgan also went along to meet Richard.

One day Richard said to Joyce, "Aren't you going to wish me a happy birthday?"

As they talked about the special occasion, he told Joyce he hadn't spoken to his mother in years.

"Oh, Richard, the Bible says that before you were born the Lord knew all about you," Joyce told him. "You are special to Him and I know your mother is thinking about you today. I'm going to give you a hug for her."

As she hugged him, Richard's eyes filled with tears.

"I'll be back later with a present for you," Joyce told him.

When she returned, she brought Richard a Bible. He received it and thanked her warmly.

Later in the week, Joyce and a friend stopped by Richard's booth. When she didn't see Richard, Joyce asked the attendant where he was. Hearing her voice,

Richard stepped out from behind the service area.

"Give that lady an onion," he said, "and add a Coke to go."

Leola

One year, Joyce visited Leola, the Little Lady at the Fair. As she bought her ticket, she learned that the man selling it was Leola's cousin. She found out his name was Arus and that the two were from Haiti.

Joyce gave Arus a Bible and visited him each day.

One day she asked him, "Why do you do this?"

"We are so poor in Haiti," he answered. "I have six children. I do this six months each year to feed my wife and children."

The next year, Leola and Arus were back at the fair and when Arus saw Joyce, he reached into his pocket and pulled out the Bible she had given him. She noticed it was worn and dog-eared.

"I read it every day this year," he told her, smiling widely.

"When I go to the fair, I just let things happen; I can't make them happen," Joyce says. When she thinks about Liz, she considers how important it is for parents to pray for their children. When she remembers all her fair friends, she knows they were divine appointments and she's quick to give God the glory.

Note: Although in the future people will no longer be placed on exhibition at the fair, Joyce anticipates there will still be many opportunities to share Jesus and looks forward to what God will continue to do.

CHAPTER NINE

LITTLE ORPHAN ANNIE

They called her Little Orphan Annie because her story paralleled that of the comic strip character. Few other residents have had as much impact on The Lighthouse family.

When Annie was seven, her mother (whom we'll call Louise) entered New Life for Girls. She was expecting her fourth child. Annie and her two sisters were staying with relatives.

Louise eventually came to The Lighthouse, had another daughter and moved back to New Life. But after a short while, she called, asking if she could bring her family to live at The Lighthouse. For the sake of the children, Joyce and Morgan consented to let her come, and for more than a year Louise, the baby, Annie, and another of Annie's sisters (the fourth lived with her grandmother) occupied the basement family room. While they were there, Joyce tried to help Louise develop parenting skills. However, most of the care of the children fell on Joyce. Eventually, Louise found a furnished apartment and Morgan and Joyce were hopeful that she would finally take responsibility for her family. They were soon to learn, though, that she was back to her old life on the streets. They tried to keep in contact with the older children through their grandmother, helping her whenever they could, but they eventually lost all contact.

Again after about a year, Louise called and asked Joyce and Morgan if they would take Annie. They agreed that they would, made a room ready, bought her some clothes and enrolled her at Christian School of York. But after they informed the welfare office of Annie's change of address, they received a call from an enraged Louise who had just learned that her monthly welfare payments were being reduced. She soon showed up to take Annie back.

Each time Annie left, there were tears. This time, several Oriental girls living at The Lighthouse devised a plan for her to stay in touch. They put Joyce and Morgan's phone number on a piece of paper, placed it in her shoe and told her to use it anytime she needed help. Annie used it more than once.

Over a period of eighteen years Annie moved in and out of The Lighthouse many times, often staying there when her mother was in prison. Sometimes Joyce and Morgan picked her up at her grandmother's, once they flew her in from California, and once drove to Philadelphia to bring her "home." Every time she called, her room was made ready and clothing was purchased. She was enrolled at Christian School of York on several occasions. Once she attended for only a week.

Annie, Morgan and Joyce and their children never stopped hoping that every arrival would be "for good." But their hopes were always dashed when Louise showed up and took Annie away. Each farewell became harder than the one before.

Joyce had talked with Annie on a number of occasions about accepting Jesus and once Annie had prayed and asked Jesus to come into her heart. When Joyce and Morgan arranged for her to attend their church camp one summer, she had "gone to the altar" there. But when Louise brought Annie to The Lighthouse for her fifteenth birthday and allowed her to spend the following week there, she committed her life more completely to the Lord. Again, when the week was up, she didn't want to leave.

"Someday," Joyce told her, "when you are old enough to make the decision, you may come back to stay."

Six years later the phone rang.

It was Annie.

"Joyce, do you remember you said I could come back when I'm old enough to make my own decisions?" she asked. "Did you mean that?"

That's the call that took Joyce and Morgan to Philadelphia.

They remember finding the address Annie had given them and seeing her sitting on the steps of an apartment house with all her earthly possessions piled beside her.

"She ran toward the car; I jumped out and we hugged," Joyce says. "We were so happy. She was twenty-one and we hadn't seen each other since she was fifteen."

When Annie had been back at The Lighthouse about a year, Joyce experienced a flare-up of her Multiple Sclerosis (chapter 26). During that previous year, Annie had followed Joyce like a shadow and knew the routine of The Lighthouse perfectly.

"She was such a help to me," Joyce recalls.

When that crisis was past, Morgan and Joyce encouraged Annie to look for a job so she would have health insurance. She was soon hired by a nursing home; Morgan took her to work and picked her up each day.

After she had worked for ninety days, Annie began to receive health benefits. She had been working about four months by Thanksgiving Day. Steve and Amy were home from Africa that year, and Morgan and Joyce had gone to their house for dinner. Annie had to work but they had assured her that her dinner would be waiting when she was finished. Before that time, though, the phone rang. It was Annie and she was crying.

"This is a bummer that I have to work today," she said.

Then she told them she had fallen while emptying trash.

That was the beginning of Annie's final journey. After a number of tests, she was diagnosed with Wilson's Disease, a rare and debilitating illness. Soon, she was a patient at the home where she had been employed. Her body became twisted and she could do nothing for herself. Her former co-workers cared for her lovingly. Once a month she was transported by ambulance to a research hospital for evaluation and treatment. Joyce always accompanied her. During the trips they came to know the emergency medical technicians and the staff members at the hospital. Because Annie was unable to speak, Joyce told them her story.

"It's my mouth but it's your story," she told Annie.

Every EMT got a New Testament and Joyce was given permission to set up a table at the hospital and distribute testaments to the nurses.

Before her illness, Annie exhibited a missionary heart. One Christmas Eve she said to Joyce, "Don't you wish we could bring all the homeless kids here and give them popcorn and hot chocolate?"

When a missionary conference was held at their church, Annie dressed in a national costume and carried the flag of that country. It was a highlight of her life.

Annie always loved and admired Amy. One day she said to Joyce, "I wanted to be a missionary just like Amy."

Joyce told her she already was a missionary.

Annie celebrated her twenty-fifth birthday at the nursing home. A group of young women from the church helped to make it a special occasion. When she learned that she was going to be admitted to the hospital in December of that year, she had one of the girls at The Lighthouse take her to the local Wal-Mart, where she rode a motorized cart and bought Christmas gifts for Joyce and Morgan. Shortly after that, she died.

Morgan and Joyce provided a place for her in their family burial plot and after a discussion with her aunt, the one family member who had shown genuine interest in Annie, had the words *Peace at Last* put on her tombstone. Her mother came to her funeral high on drugs.

Morgan describes Annie's life, aside from her times at The Lighthouse, as one of physical and mental abuse.

"She never felt secure in her own family," he says.

Annie *did* feel secure at The Lighthouse. There, she knew she was loved.

CHAPTER TEN

SANDIP AND FRIENDS

J oyce's words fall over each other when she talks about Sandip.

"Sandip was very compassionate. He was studying to be a doctor. He knew where he wanted to go. He became an instant member of the family."

Sandip, a Hindu from India, and Johannes, a Christian from Ethiopia, were roommates at The Lighthouse during a very multi-cultured period. Jaffery, a devout Muslim, was in the room next to them. Chully, a Buddhist from Ski Lanka and Marise, a Roman Catholic from Haiti, were in the third bedroom on the same level of the house. Pyush, another Hindu, lived in the basement. All were attending York College. Sandip was the respected leader of the group.

"Can you imagine our kitchen in the mornings with all those people getting ready for the day?"

Joyce says, laughing.

Likewise, dinner presented an interesting picture.

"Every night, we joined hands around the table and Morgan prayed," Joyce remembered fondly. "I always put a lot of effort into our dinnertime. I wanted it to be special. It was the only time we all sat down together."

Although Jaffery faithfully observed the Muslim prayer ritual five times a day, he appeared to be searching for truth. He and Joyce often had long discussions about spiritual things and occasionally he would join her for devotions. She remembers the night she heard his whispered call from the stairway outside her bedroom.

"Joyce, are you sleeping?"

She went out.

"Joyce, I now believe that Jesus is the Messiah," he told her.

Shortly after that, Jaffery moved from the area.

Sharkar (Sharky) entered this melting pot about a year later. He, too, was from India. Joyce met him at an international dinner at the college. When Sharky was introduced to Jesus at the college pub by two men who were involved in Evangelism Explosion, he rode a bicycle to The Lighthouse to tell Joyce and Morgan he had accepted Christ. When he became dissatisfied with his housing situation a short time later, he contacted them and soon joined The Lighthouse family.

Joyce remembers the day she put the map of the world on the kitchen wall.

"You should have seen the residents when they came home," she says. "They were so touched. They gathered around to show us where they were from."

That night Joyce found a note by her plate at the dinner table.

It said, "Thank you for putting up the map."

Sandip came to The Lighthouse while Beth and Jonas were still there. He and Yohannes were both in their wedding.

"Yohannes was also very special to us," Joyce explained. "He and Sandip were like brothers. Anytime Yohannes was going on a trip, he would kneel in front of Morgan and say, 'Bless me before I leave.'"

Returning to Sandip, Joyce said, "He was one of the joy bells of The Lighthouse. It was really fun having him here."

She recalled how he would always notice anything she had done, any changes she'd made. He was also quick to lend a helping hand.

"If I was vacuuming and he came in, he'd say, 'Here, I'll finish it.'"

Sandip stayed in close touch with Joyce and Morgan after he left for medical school. One day he told them that his father had arranged for him to return to India to pick out a wife. He said five women had been chosen, and he would have tea and spend time with each before making his decision. Sandip was not comfortable with this arrangement but felt he must obey his father.

"How will I know?" he asked Joyce nervously.

"Sandip, you will just know," she told him. "I will be praying that you know."

Sandip did know when he met Ami. He soon married her and returned to finish his medical training. Ami made a trip to America and met Joyce and Morgan, but went back to India to finish her education.

"Just think. Someday you will be a doctor," Joyce once told Sandip. "Maybe you'll even take care of me."

"If you ever need my services, you know I'll take care of you," he replied.

Today Sandip and Ami are both doctors in North Carolina and have a baby son. Recently Joyce e-mailed Sandip on his birthday and received this reply:

I was pleasantly surprised to get your e-greeting. Thanks.

Thank you very much for the update. With such a large family and an even larger extended family, it is awesome that you keep up with everything.

Ami and I are fine. Ami has started her own private practice and I have been with this group in Radiology for 4 years. I will become a partner in July this year.

Hope you can come on down and visit us here.

I keep telling Ami and our family members, that my two years at your place were the foundation for my career. I could not find a better role model than Morgan. Thank you, Morgan. Morgan's character and Joyce, your outlook for life are worth emulating. Whatever little of that I have tried to practice has been very satisfying.

Thank you,

Love,

Sandip

Author's note: Shortly after that communication, I had the privilege of accompanying Joyce and Shonna on a visit to Sandip and Ami's home. Joyce and Sandip had not seen each other for fifteen years and the reunion between them was moving. Their reminiscences, as we had dinner, were captivating. Although I tried to stay in the background, Sandip and Ami's gracious hospitality drew me into the circle of friendship.

Among my memories of the evening is a statement from Ami.

"Tell Morgan thank you for me," she said to Joyce. "He taught Sandip to be a husband. In India the men say, 'do this' and 'do this' (gesturing with her hands). Sandip does not do that."

As I watched Ami and Sandip together, I knew that Sandip had learned his lessons well.

CHAPTER ELEVEN

JOHN MORGAN

It was October. Joyce was handing out Bibles at the county prison when she saw the two girls, one of whom was braiding the other's hair.

"Don't give them one," the chaplain said. "They're from Africa and don't speak English."

When Amy and Steve were home from Côte d'Ivoire the previous summer, a friend asked Amy to accompany her to a craft class at the prison, explaining that a girl from Africa was attending the class. When Amy met the girl, she greeted her in Jula, the language of the people with whom they had worked, and the girl's eyes lit up. It was her native tongue. Amy visited with Fatu* several times after that and when the time came for them to return to Africa, she and Steve went to the prison to say goodbye. They left one of their prayer cards with her.

Joyce had checked out of the prison and was on her way to the car when the idea struck.

"I wonder if one of those two girls could have been the girl from Côte d'Ivoire Amy told me about."

She turned around, walked to the entrance and found a guard.

"Could I go back in?" she asked.

"No," the guard said, "that's not allowed."

"Oh please," Joyce persisted. "I want to find out if one of two girls I saw in there might be from Côte d'Ivoire. My daughter is a missionary over there. I have to talk to those girls."

Acknowledging that there was a female prisoner from Côte d'Ivoire, the guard relented and led Joyce to the room where she had seen the girls. They were still there.

"Côte d'Ivoire," Joyce said, getting their attention.

"Ah-h-h," one replied, her eyes growing large.

"Daughter. . . missionary. M-i-s-s-i-o-n-a-r-y," Joyce said slowly.

"One minute," the girl replied in broken English, walking to a nearby cot.

She reached under a pillow and pulled out a card. It was Amy and Steve's prayer card.

Holding Amy's picture against Joyce's face, she said with tears running down her cheeks, "Ah. Same face. Same face."

She stroked Joyce's face and then the picture, and Joyce's tears mingled with hers.

Karen and Doug Conkle, co-workers with Amy and Steve in West Africa, came to York later that year. Karen also went to the craft class and met Fatu.

At the end of February, Karen called Joyce.

"Doug is on a missionary tour in California," she explained, "and I'm leaving to join him. Do you remember the African girl at the prison?"

Without waiting for an answer she continued.

"She's very pregnant and needs a place to live or they will put her baby in foster care."

Joyce thought about Morgan and the fact that he was scheduled to have surgery. The timing was not good.

After talking with Karen, she explained the situation to Morgan, and asked, "What do you think?"

"How can we not take her?" Morgan replied. "Our daughter is working in Côte d'Ivoire and there's someone from Côte d'Ivoire on our doorstep. Don't worry about me. I'll be fine."

Soon, Joyce was picking up Fatu at the prison, having stopped at Karen's for a French Bible. From the time they arrived home until Fatu went to the hospital, the two read the whole Gospel of John, a sentence at a time—Joyce in English, Fatu in French.

When they came to the story of the crucifixion, Fatu began to weep. Then, with Joyce's assistance, she bowed her head and invited Jesus into her life.

Later she told Joyce, "If my baby is a boy, I'm going to name him John Morgan—John after Jesus' beloved apostle and Morgan after Morgan."

Morgan's surgery went well and the day after he was discharged from the hospital, Fatu went into labor. Again, Morgan assured Joyce that he was all right, and Joyce stayed with Fatu until John Morgan was born. Two days later, Fatu and John Morgan came home and Joyce put her nursing skills to work on all three of them.

In time, Fatu told Joyce and Morgan her story.

Her husband was a newspaper reporter. He had written a story about an African prison in which twenty-nine officials died during a political uprising. The prison attributed their deaths to cholera, but Fatu's husband and two other reporters suspected foul play. Because of threats on their lives, the three fled the country, one to England, one to Canada, and Fatu's husband to the United States—all with illegal passports. Fatu's husband was arrested and put in a New Jersey prison.

Soon afterwards, police arrived at Fatu's home in Côte d'Ivoire, ransacking it and taking a camera. They questioned Fatu about her husband's where-abouts and arrested her when she wouldn't disclose it. A member of her family located her in jail and gave a guard twenty-five dollars to turn his head while she escaped. Using a cousin's passport, Fatu came to New York where she was soon arrested and put in prison—the same prison where her husband was detained.

One day Fatu became ill in prison and cried out in her native Jula. A guard, who knew she was from Côte d'Ivoire, recalled "an African guy" who might be able to interpret. He brought Fatu's husband to her, and when the two saw each other, they could not hide their surprise. Fatu's husband spoke in French, "This is my wife!" Fatu answered, "This is my husband!"

The guards, who were skeptical, placed them in separate rooms and asked identical questions. When they gave the same answers, the guards were convinced they were husband and wife and allowed them to spend the night together. John Morgan was conceived that night. The next day a prison riot necessitated moving the prisoners to other facilities. Fatu was sent to York and her husband to a prison in another county.

Some time later, Fatu again became ill. When this illness continued, she was seen by a doctor who determined that she was pregnant.

Fatu wrote to her husband, telling him of the pregnancy and giving him Amy and Steve's address in Côte d'Ivoire. Fatu's husband was deported to Africa the day before his case was scheduled to be presented by an attorney.

One day Amy answered a knock on her door in Côte d'Ivoire to find a disheveled man claiming to be Fatu's husband. He begged her for information about his wife.

Amy, who knew where she was, replied, "Don't worry. Your wife is with my mother in America. She will take good care of her."

One morning shortly after John Morgan was born, while Joyce and Fatu were eating breakfast, the phone rang. It was Amy telling her mother to put Fatu on the phone and set the timer for ten minutes.

"Her husband is here," Amy explained. "This is

my gift to them. It is costing ten dollars a minute."

Fatu took the phone and heard her husband say, "I want to congratulate you on our son." Amy had given him the news.

After he had talked to his wife, Amy gave Fatu's husband some food and he slipped away, still fearing for his life. He called Fatu once after that, but the call was cut off. Then her mother received word that he had been killed.

Fatu received a six-month's humanitarian leave from prison to care for her son. During that time, a sympathetic attorney arranged for her to leave the country. A year later, her "dead" husband located her in her new home. They have since had another child and are reunited with a daughter who had been living with Fatu's mother in Africa.

At least twice a year, near Christmas and Easter, Fatu calls. When Morgan answers the phone, the conversation is about John Morgan. When Joyce answers, Fatu says, "Hello, Joyce. This is Fatu. I just want to tell you I love you. You will always be my family."

*Not real name

CHAPTER TWELVE

NURSING

The gift of a nurse's kit when she was five years old set Joyce's course for the future; but her childhood dream was almost shattered the day her father told her there was no money for her education. An English teacher who learned of her situation kept the dream alive by convincing the Professional Business Women's Club to award her an interest-free loan to attend nursing school.

Joyce credits Morgan with the fact that she finished the program. When she once talked of quitting to get married, he stated, "I'm not going to answer to Charlie Miller (Joyce's dad). You wanted to be a nurse long before you met me and that's what you're going to be."

"I've always been grateful to Morgan, and Morgan has always been grateful for my nursing," Joyce says. "It has played an important part in our family and in our ministry."

Nursing, of course, is what brought Joyce into contact with Claude Banks, whose house became The Lighthouse.

When the last of the four Ilgenfritz children left the nest, Joyce went to work in a doctor's office. Although it often stretches her already busy schedule, the part-time work provides another mission field. The doctor, who is a Christian, allows her to talk freely with patients about spiritual matters.

Robert* was one of those patients. He was overweight. Once, as Joyce was checking him in, Robert said, "I'm so unhappy with myself. When I look in the mirror, all I see are double chins."

"Did anyone ever tell you you're special?" Joyce asked him. "Do you know that Jesus loves you?"

Just then, the doctor appeared in the doorway and Joyce left to assume other duties. When he finished his exam, the doctor told Joyce to go back in and talk to Robert. Entering the room, she saw him arranging a row of pictures on the examining table. They were his driver's licenses from the last twenty years.

"Why Robert, these are all you!" Joyce exclaimed.

"Yeah," he replied dejectedly.

Joyce looked intently at the pictures, then pointed to the last five.

"If I'd be stranded along the highway and these five men came along, I'd choose this one," she said, indicating the most recent one.

"Why do you say that?" Robert asked.

"Because this one has kind eyes," Joyce replied.

"If I have kind eyes, I got them from my grandmother. She's been praying for me since I was a little boy," Robert responded.

"Are you a Christian, Robert?" Joyce asked.

"If you're asking me if I'm born again, no, I'm not," he said.

"Well, you're not yet, but I feel God has something special for you," Joyce told him, pulling a New Testament out of her pocket. "I'd like to give you a little present."

Robert took the testament without hesitation and listened as Joyce showed him the plan of salvation in the back and explained how he could pray and receive Jesus as his Savior.

"And, Robert," she instructed finally, "when you get home, I want you to call your grandmother and tell her a nurse gave you a Bible today."

David* and Dianne* were regular patients. One day David called and said Dianne was really sick. When he brought her into the office it was obvious her condition was serious. The doctor sent her to the hospital where she was examined by an emergency room physician. During the examination, Dianne asked, "Doctor, if I was your mother, what would you do with me?"

"I'd send you home to die," the physician replied.

"Then do it," Dianne said.

When this news reached the doctor's office, Joyce couldn't get Dianne out of her mind. At the end of the day, she called her. When Dianne told

Joyce about her conversation with the emergency room physician, Joyce asked, "Dianne, what do you know about heaven?"

"I don't know anything," Dianne replied.

"Could I come to your house and tell you about it?" Joyce inquired.

When Dianne said yes, Joyce quickly made a salad to take along and left for her house, praying all the way. As they talked, she concluded that Dianne's knowledge of heaven was limited to the Christmas and Easter stories. So she explained God's plan for His children to spend eternity with Him.

"It sounds wonderful," Dianne said, "but I could never go to heaven. I'm not good enough."

Then Dianne began to tell Joyce about the sinful lives she and David had led, a lifestyle that had led them to divorce, and then eventually to remarry.

"Oh, Dianne, that's why Jesus died," Joyce exclaimed.

As they continued the discussion, David listened intently. Eventually, he and Dianne both prayed and asked Christ to come into their hearts.

For the next three weeks, David sat by Dianne's bed, reading aloud from the New Testament Joyce had given her. Finally Dianne closed her eyes and went to be with Jesus.

When Joyce went to Dianne's viewing, she encountered Dianne's son, whose relationship with his mother had been strained. Dianne's granddaughter was with her father. Joyce introduced herself and shared how Dianne had prayed and asked God to forgive her sins.

"We all need to forgive one another," she added.

With tears running down her cheeks, Dianne's granddaughter asked, "Did my grandmother *really* accept Jesus into her life?"

Evelyn* and Gary* were also regular patients. Evelyn, too, was very ill. When she was sent to the hospital from the office one day, Joyce whispered in her ear and told her to say Jesus the whole way there.

Some time later, Evelyn returned to the office and informed Joyce, "I did what you told me."

Joyce asked Evelyn and Gary if she could come to visit them.

"Evelyn, what would have happened if you had not made it to the hospital?" she inquired as they sat around the dining room table.

"Well, I hope I would have gone to heaven," Evelyn replied.

Again, Joyce shared God's plan for salvation and both Evelyn and Gary prayed to receive Christ.

"Isn't it wonderful that you both now know that you will see each other again when something happens to one of you?" Joyce asked.

One day Evelyn called the office to tell them that Gary had died.

"Do you remember the day you and Gary prayed to receive Christ?" Joyce asked her.

"That's what's carrying me through," Evelyn responded.

Ten-year-old Patty* was not the patient the first time she and her mother came to the office.

"Young lady, why aren't you in school?" Joyce asked her.

"I want to see what the doctor says about my mother," Patty replied.

Patty's concern for her mother was well-founded, and as Joyce talked with them about their destructive lifestyles, Patty prayed to receive Christ.

The two came to the office several times over the next three years. However, they continued to make poor decisions, and when Patty was thirteen, her mother brought her in for a pregnancy test. Joyce wasn't working that day, nor was she there when the doctor called to tell them it was positive. But she was disturbed when he told her afterwards that Patty's mother would not discuss anything but an abortion.

The next time she worked, Joyce called Patty's mother.

"Joyce, I don't even want to hear what you have to say," she quickly informed her. "I have my mind made up."

"I just called to tell you there's a place for Patty to go where she can continue her schooling until she has the baby," Joyce replied.

Then she asked to talk to Patty.

"Do you want an abortion?" she asked her.

"No," Patty replied.

Joyce told her about the nearby maternity home.

"I want to go there," Patty said.

Finally, Patty's mother agreed to visit the home and arrangements were made for Patty to await her baby's birth there.

On Sanctity of Life Sunday the following

January, Patty gave birth to a boy. Her mother and Joyce were with her.

After she held her grandson for the first time, Patty's mother turned to Joyce and asked, "How can I ever thank you?"

That same day, Joyce learned that one of her high school teachers, who was also one of their patients, was on another floor. For some reason, he always greeted Joyce with sarcasm when he came to the office and Joyce did not enjoy his visits.

"At first it was funny," she recalled, "but then it really started to bother me. One day I asked him if I had ever done anything to offend him. I told him if I had, I was sorry."

After that, their conversations improved a bit.

"You're not getting any younger," Joyce told him once. "It's about time you begin to think about some serious things."

The last time they talked in the office, Joyce asked him if he knew where he was going when he died. Again, the sarcasm surfaced and he told her he was going to hell to be with all his friends.

Now he was dying and Joyce knew he was just a floor above where she was waiting with Patty's family. She excused herself and went to his room. Much to her surprise, he was receptive to everything she shared with him and before she left, he prayed to receive Christ.

As she left the hospital that night, Joyce marveled.

"Here it is, Lord, Sanctity of Life Sunday and You have brought a new life into the world and saved the soul of a man near the end of his journey. Oh, thank You, Lord Jesus."

Ronald* came to the office often. One day he told Joyce he felt like he had a big hole in his heart.

"Ronald, you know what? You do have a big hole in your heart. The only way to fill it is to let Jesus come into it."

Ronald never came to the office after that without mentioning the hole. Sometimes he would say it was smaller; other times, bigger.

One day Ronald's wife called and said he was in the hospital and was not expected to live. Joyce went to the hospital. As soon as he saw her, Ronald spoke.

"I know what you're going to ask me," he said. "I want you to know the hole is closed."

Joyce took Ronald's hand and prayed for him. Then she kissed him on the cheek.

"Thank you for not giving up on me," Ronald said.

He died a short time later.

Charlie* had a terminal illness.

One evening the doctor called Joyce and asked her to come in early the next day.

"Charlie is coming in," he said. "I don't know where he stands with the Lord and I want you to talk to him."

Before Joyce left the house the next morning, she picked up a New Testament. She prayed the whole way to work.

"Lord, what am I going to say to him?" she asked.

"I've known Charlie for years and he's never shown any interest in spiritual things."

When she checked Charlie in, Joyce noted his weight loss.

"Charlie, you're a very sick man," she said.

"I know," he said. "I'm going to die."

"Charlie, do you know where you will go when you die?" Joyce asked.

"Well nurse, nobody knows that," Charlie replied.

"O yes," Joyce said. "Either you will go to heaven or you will go to hell."

"I want to go to heaven, but I don't know how to get there," Charlie said.

Joyce pulled the New Testament out of her pocket and showed Charlie the verses about heaven. Then she asked if he would like to pray and invite Jesus into his heart.

"I would," Charlie replied.

After he prayed, Charlie asked Joyce for a pen and with a shaking hand wrote his name and the date in the New Testament and put it in his pocket.

Soon the doctor came into the room.

"Charlie, you're smiling," he said.

"I'm smiling because I know I'm going to heaven when I die," Charlie told him.

"How do you know?" the doctor asked.

"Because I have proof right here," Charlie replied, pulling out the testament.

Soon after that Charlie died. A couple weeks later, his mother and brother came into the office. As his mother sat on the same chair Charlie had recently occupied, Joyce felt compelled to tell her about what had occurred during Charlie's last visit.

"On this very chair..." she began.

When she finished, Charlie's mother said, "I have prayed for Charlie for years."

Then she looked at Joyce's nametag as if seeing it for the first time.

"Joyce!" she said. "Right before Charlie died, he said 'Joyce' a number of times. I didn't know who Joyce was, but now I do."

Charlie's brother looked just like him. Joyce asked him if he knew he was going to see Charlie when he died. He confessed that he didn't, but promised to think about it.

Joyce reflects on these persons, and others.

"Whenever I feel like retiring, this is what keeps me going," she says. "There are so many hurting people out there. Sometimes they just need to know somebody cares."

*Not real name

CHAPTER THIRTEEN

PRISON MINISTRIES

April 13, 2000—journal entry:

What a privilege to be used by Jesus today. We gave out 140 English testaments, plus 24 Spanish and two Russian. I hugged so many girls in Jesus' name—girls from Africa, Santo Domingo, China, Brazil, Uganda, Ukraine, Puerto Rico, and the USA.

Lord, they all received a copy of Your Word. You know each one by name. Do a miracle in their lives in Jesus' name. Amen.

One of Joyce's favorite things to do is give out Bibles at the York County Prison. Representing the Auxiliary of Gideon's International, she and a female partner take two hundred testaments to the facility twice a year—once in the spring and again in the fall. When they arrive at the prison, they are escorted into a large room surrounded by pods (cells).

"The chaplain always announces, 'The Gideon ladies are here and they have a gift for you,' as the detainees file into the gym," Joyce explains. "I show them the testaments and point out the plan of salvation in the back. Then, as the chaplain calls names, we put a testament in each hand. They have the right to refuse one, but few do."

Joyce explained her personal motivation.

"I go to speak words of encouragement. Some of them just made bad choices. I try to think what their lives were like. I give every single girl a hug and kiss," she continued. "I call them Jesus hugs. I say their name and then add 'Jesus loves you. No matter what you've done, He will forgive you.'"

On a recent visit, the prison chaplain reminded Joyce that at least one-third of the women have sexually transmitted diseases or AIDS.

"I pray for protection before I go," she explains. "If that's the way the Lord chooses to take me home to be with Him, it's all right with me."

On one occasion, Joyce and two Gideon sisters arrived at the prison, each carrying a large basket of testaments. They were ushered to a room which was already occupied by two men in business suits. While they waited for the guard to open the gate, Joyce asked the men if they would like a copy of God's Word. To her surprise, they both said yes. Then the correctional officer came and let them in. The chaplain soon arrived and took them to her office, apologizing for not being at the gate to meet them. Seated on a chair next to the chaplain's desk was a beautiful young woman with long, brown hair. She was dressed in an orange jump suit, had her hands over her face and was sobbing uncontrollably.

"This is Tammy,"* the chaplain said to the ladies. "Tammy just got very bad news."

Turning to the girl, the chaplain explained that the women were Christians who knew how to pray and asked if she could share the news with them. Tammy nodded affirmatively.

"Tammy just learned that she is HIV Positive," the chaplain went on, as Tammy began crying loudly.

Joyce went to Tammy, put her arms around her and held her tightly. "Jesus, please help Tammy," she prayed.

After a few minutes Tammy calmed down and the ladies gave her a Bible and explained God's plan to her. Then a prison officer arrived and told her that her parole officers were waiting to see her. Later, Joyce learned that the parole officers were the two men who had accepted Bibles in the waiting room.

Gerry* was on hall duty when Joyce visited the prison on another occasion.

"Gerry, tell Joyce what just happened to you," the chaplain suggested.

Gerry quickly related that she had just accepted Jesus. Then she started to cry. "But I'm so sad," she explained, following Joyce's hug and words of encouragement. "My mother is dying and doesn't know the Lord."

When Joyce learned that Gerry's mother was in a local nursing home, she promised to visit her after leaving the prison.

Entering the woman's room later in the day, Joyce explained, "Mrs. Brown,* you don't know me but I just visited your daughter, Gerry."

"Oh, how is she?" the woman asked quietly.

"Well, I came to bring you a special message from her," Joyce explained. "Gerry invited Jesus into her heart and asked Him to forgive her of her sins, and she's concerned about you. You are very sick and she wants to be sure she will see you in heaven."

The two women continued in conversation and before long Mrs. Brown prayed to receive Jesus. Joyce called Gerry later in the day (as pre-arranged with the chaplain) and relayed the good news.

When Joyce left the nursing home, she asked the attendant to call her if Gerry's mother's condition worsened. When the call came, Joyce hurried back to the home, only to learn that Mrs. Brown had just died. Joyce cried tears of joy because she knew she was with Jesus.

In the days following Gerry's mother's death, Joyce pondered what she could do for Gerry. Finally, she received special permission from the chaplain at the prison to bring a pastor to conduct a memorial service in the chaplain's office. At the appointed time, a number of girls in orange jump suits filed into the office.

The pastor asked Gerry to share her testimony and tell about her mother's salvation. Then he spoke about the two thieves on the cross. When he completed with, "Remember me this day..." fourteen girls prayed to receive Christ.

A young female prisoner who was to be released the next day accepted her testament reluctantly. That night, her cellmate, who was a Christian, read to her from it and she accepted Christ. Not long after she was released, she died in a house fire.

In the aftermath of her death, the girl's mother talked with an insurance man who was a Gideon; he offered her a Bible.

"I have one," she responded. "My daughter got one in prison and accepted Christ. I have hers."

Sometimes the visits have a lighter side. An inmate named Susan* approached Joyce to receive her testament.

"I remember your perfume," she said smiling. "Maybe it will rub off on me. I want to smell like you smell."

"I don't want a Bible," another woman said. "I just want a hug."

Sometimes the women will say they don't want a Bible and after a hug and word of encouragement, they change their minds and ask for a Bible.

Once, Joyce went into a bathroom and found a girl brushing her teeth. Joyce offered her a Bible. She replied, "No, thank you. I am a Muslim. Do you have the Koran?"

"No, I am sorry, I don't," Joyce replied, "but

may I give you a hug?"

Joyce held her in her arms and whispered into her ear how special she was and how much God loved her.

When Joyce and the other ladies were getting ready to leave the area, the girl came running up to them.

"Do you have any Bibles left?" she asked. "I would love to have one."

"That day was wonderful," Joyce recorded afterwards. "Many of the correctional officers asked if they could have Bibles and several even asked if they could have one for their children at home. Before we left, we had a time of prayer in the chaplain's office. We prayed for a mighty movement of God in the prison."

Morgan ministers to men in the prison; he and his Gideon brothers also take testaments to local military bases and Bibles to hotels and motels.

"The greatest thing you're offering is hope," he says. "I always tell the men, 'You've got to read what's in this little book. Don't just take it, but read it.'"

Joyce often encourages the women to write prayer requests for her to take home.

"The most heartbreaking prayer (and the most frequent)," she says, "is 'Please pray for my children.'"

Once, after she had prayed with a woman for her daughter and son, Joyce sent her a note on paper that had a teacup on the front. The woman sent back a picture of a teacup she had drawn. Checking out of a local store months later, Joyce heard the question, "Do you remember me?"

It was her teacup friend.

"The Scripture about visiting those in prison has taken on new meaning for me," Joyce said recently. "Every time I go to the prison, I feel such compassion. I can't explain it.

"Some people have to be down and out before they can hear from God," she continued. "We go in the name of Jesus and He loves the prisoners through us."

*Not real name

Note: Throughout the book, "Bible," "New Testament," and "Testament" are used interchangeably. Among other ministries, the Gideons and their wives (the Auxiliary) distribute New Testaments in prisons and place Bibles in hotels, motels, schools, and health facilities.

Morgan and Joyce – Keepers of the Lighthouse

Family outing at Mark's farm

Morgan, Joyce and Shonna celebrating Grandma
Helen's 95th birthday

Mark, Miriam and children

Beth, Ashley, Amee and Jonas

Grandma (Joyce) with her "Stars of the Week"
at the beach

Kari, Peter and Abby welcoming Miyuki to
America

"Our Fair Lady"

Sandip and Morgan

CHAPTER FOURTEEN

CAMPUS CLUBS

It never dawned on Joyce to ask permission. She just awoke during the night with the idea and got up and collected all the memorabilia that Japanese houseguests had given her over the years. The next morning, she went across the street to the York College campus. She put up a table, arranged the items and added a sign inviting all foreign students to a picnic at The Lighthouse the following week. It was only later, when someone questioned her, that she realized it might have been a good idea to check with the college first.

Thirty-five students came to the picnic! It was the beginning of the International Club which continues at York College twenty-five years later. Miyuki, the most recent Japanese student to live at The Lighthouse, served as vice-president during her senior year.

The picnics to welcome new foreign students are

still held at The Lighthouse each fall, and every year Joyce and Morgan attend an international dinner sponsored by the group.

Tomie attended the first picnic. She had just come to the college and was very homesick. She and Amy became friends and Tomie spent her first Christmas away from home at The Lighthouse. Amy eventually led her to the Lord and she attended church with the family during the rest of her stay in the United States. On her last Sunday before returning to Japan, the pastor prayed for her and presented her with a Bible.

While the International Club served its purpose on the college campus, Joyce was still burdened for the spiritual condition of the students. So she began to ask the Lord for two students to start a Bible study. For six weeks she walked around the college dormitories and prayed.

A former houseguest from New Life for Girls was the first one to express interest. She brought a friend to the initial meeting. God had provided two students.

Joyce taught the study for a time and it grew in number. Just when it was becoming burdensome to serve as both hostess and teacher, the Lord provided another teacher. Since the class was going well, Joyce was disappointed when he told her after a short time that he was moving from the area.

Faced with not having a teacher and not wanting to dissolve the group, Joyce sought the Lord again.

As she was kneeling in prayer one day, the doorbell rang. It was a local minister, offering to help.

Under his leadership, the group outgrew Joyce's dining room, and the college agreed to give them a room in which to meet. When a man from a nearby college campus introduced InterVarsity, a national Christian organization for college students, the group embraced its tenets and InterVarsity came to the York College campus.

Recently, Joyce had an opportunity to share the beginnings of the InterVarsity Club with about seventy members, many of whom (including her grandson Seth and Miyuki) participate in both the International Club and InterVarsity.

One of Joyce's favorite sayings is "bloom where you are planted." She and Morgan were obviously planted across the street from a mission field and they have bloomed there. So have many of the students whose lives they've touched.

CHAPTER FIFTEEN

AIRPLANE ADVENTURES

"I love airports," Joyce confesses. "I love to be where there are people. Many people are so empty and sad. I just love to look at them and smile."

Once, Joyce recorded the following prayer in her journal.

Dear Father, keep me still to hear Your voice. Make me sensitive to the needs of the people with whom I come in contact. Give me boldness to witness to the power of the gospel. Lord, I pray for divine appointments to tell someone of Your transforming power. In Jesus' name, help me not to miss one opportunity for You.

When she was on her way to Africa for Kari's birth, Joyce entered a phone booth in the airport in New York. As she dialed the number, she looked into the next booth and saw a woman dressed in African garb. Their eyes met.

"I knew right away I'd like to get to know her," she recalled.

The woman finished her conversation first and disappeared from Joyce's sight. Joyce had no idea where she was going and figured she'd never see her again.

Soon Joyce was on her way to Belgium. During a seven-hour delay in the airport there, she found herself looking for the lady. Once, she thought she saw her but lost her in the crowds. She finally boarded in Belgium and walked to her seat. There, sitting in the next seat, was the lady.

Before Joyce could speak, the lady said in excellent English, "I saw you in New York. I looked for you in Belgium and couldn't find you."

"Isn't that strange?" Joyce said. "I was looking for you, too."

The lady told Joyce her name was LaVina,* that she was with UNICEF and that she was going to Abidjan, Côte d'Ivoire. That was Joyce's destination.

When their dinner trays arrived, Joyce asked LaVina if she could pray.

"Please do," she replied.

"She was hungry for spiritual food," Joyce recalls. "I shared some Bible verses I had just memorized, and she had me write them down for her."

When Joyce's new friend guided her through customs in Abidjan, Joyce remembered a piece of paper that her sister had given her before she left on which was written, *"For he shall give his angels charge over thee, to keep thee in all thy ways"* (Psalm 91:11 KJV).

"She was the angel God sent to help me," Joyce said. "If it hadn't been for her, I don't know how I'd have gotten through that airport."

Inadvertently, Joyce's health records remained in LaVina's possession after customs. Joyce had mentioned the guesthouse where she would be staying in Abidjan and before she discovered they were missing, she received a call from LaVina.

After Kari was born, Joyce contacted her and she came to the hospital, bringing the papers and a beautiful bouquet of tropical plants for Amy.

While Amy, Joyce, and Kari were staying at the guesthouse until Amy could travel back to Bouake, LaVina had them to her home for dinner. She also invited her boss to meet them.

Eleven years later, after Amy and Steve had moved to Burkina Faso, Joyce received a call from Amy.

"Mother, you'll never believe this," she said. "Today Steve and I met LaVina's boss in Burkina."

When a call from Jonas informed Joyce and Morgan that Beth was having an emergency appendectomy, Joyce quickly made arrangements to fly to Colorado. Because of the circumstances, she had to fly standby. The first flight to Denver, after she arrived at the airport, didn't have room. While she was waiting for a second, a man walked by. There were four empty seats behind where Joyce was sitting but the man walked past them and came around to the one vacant seat beside her. He was eating an orange Popsicle.

"Boy, that looks refreshing," Joyce commented.

"It is," the man said. "I'd like to make it last till I get to San Francisco Bay. You should get one."

The man said his name was George. He was very personable, often shaking his head and laughing as Joyce spoke. Several times he replied, "That's what my mother says." After a while, he told her that when he was little, his mother had prayed for him to become a minister. He acknowledged that she was still praying for him.

"I went to church until I was eighteen," George said, "but then I took the other road and haven't been back since."

Joyce pulled out a New Testament and asked if he would take it.

"Must I make a commitment to read it if I do?" George asked.

"You don't have to make any commitment to me," she replied, "but if you get an urge, you'd better read it."

She wrote "Proverbs 3:5–6" inside the front cover of the testament and handed it to him. George looked at her in surprise.

"I can't believe it," he said. "That's my mother's favorite verse."

"When you get home," Joyce said, "I want you to call your mother and tell her you had a divine appointment at the airport today."

When it came time to for him to board his plane for Denver, George said, "I guess you're going to tell me you have faith to believe you'll get on this flight."

"Not necessarily," Joyce responded. "Only if it's God's will."

"If you don't, you'll probably say you have another divine appointment," he chided good-naturedly.

There was no room for Joyce on that flight and as she walked back from the desk, George leaned across the rope behind which he was waiting to enter the plane.

"Did you make it?" he whispered.

"No," Joyce replied. "Maybe the next one."

The next plane, three hours later, had a seat for Joyce—in first class. Her seatmate was Robert.

Joyce got comfortable and accepted the menu presented by the attendant.

When she began to circle entrées, as if she were in the hospital, Robert came to her aid.

"You don't need to circle them," he explained. "That's just to show you what they have."

"I guess you can tell I've never flown first class," Joyce laughed.

Dinner soon arrived and, as they ate, Joyce learned that Robert was a 31-year-old attorney whose work took him around the world. He was returning from Japan and London. In addition to his business contacts, he had undergone eye surgery in London. He said he had a wife and six-month-old daughter at home.

When they finished eating, Robert settled down

to nap. Joyce was waiting when he awoke.

"You must be anxious to see your wife and daughter," she said.

Robert replied affirmatively, adding that he was anxious for his wife to see him without glasses.

"Since you travel so much," Joyce said, "I bet you stay in a lot of hotels. Have you ever seen the Gideon Bibles that are placed in the nightstands?"

Robert acknowledged that he had.

"My husband and I belong to the Gideons," Joyce continued, "and I'd like to give you one of our New Testaments."

She handed him the little book and turned to the plan of salvation in the back, explaining how he could pray to invite Jesus into his heart. Robert accepted it thoughtfully and said, "I will read this. In fact, I'll not only read it, I'll read it with my wife."

On another occasion, while Joyce was waiting for Beth in the airport in Denver, she noticed a girl with a cast on her leg. She learned the girl was a flight attendant who had broken her kneecap in a motorcycle accident in which her boyfriend had been badly injured. A surgeon in Denver had treated her and she was flying back for a checkup. She mentioned that her dad was praying for her.

That was Joyce's opening.

"God spared your life," she told her.

"That's what my dad says," the girl replied.

"As a flight attendant, you must stay in a lot of hotels," Joyce commented. "Do you see the Gideon Bibles in the rooms?"

"I see them all the time," the girl replied, "and I always think I'll read one some day but never get around to it."

"I have a Gideon Bible in my purse," Joyce said, pulling out the little testament.

The girl listened while Joyce showed her the helps in the front and the plan of salvation in the back.

Just then Beth appeared and Joyce introduced the two.

"God sent your mother to me today," the girl told Beth.

Turning to Joyce, she added, "When I see those Gideon Bibles in hotel rooms from now on, I sure am going to read them."

She hugged Joyce and went on her way.

Joyce always carries New Testaments when she travels.

Recently she looked around an airport after praying, "Lord, if You want me to give this to someone, show me."

Everybody seemed to be rushing, talking on cell phones, or checking schedules.

Suddenly she saw a cleaning lady. It was as if God said, "This is the one."

"Lord, I'm not going to just walk over and give her a Bible. If You really want her to have one, bring her to me," she prayed silently.

As she watched, the lady worked her way toward her.

"You're doing a good job," Joyce said when she

got within hearing distance. "What's your name?"

"Joyce," the lady replied.

"That's my name, too," Joyce said. "What's your middle name?"

"Elaine," the cleaning lady answered.

"Oh, that's mine, too," Joyce exclaimed. "Don't tell me your birthday is June second."

"No, mine is in July," the lady replied.

"Next week at this time, I'm going to be doing what you're doing," the lady continued. "I'm treating myself to a trip to Hawaii."

"Oh, may I give you something for your trip?" Joyce asked.

As she reached into her pocketbook, she realized the lady thought she was going to give her money, so she said, "What I am going to give you is better than silver or gold."

The lady accepted the testament and listened while Joyce showed her how to use it. They hugged and the lady went on with her cleaning.

Sometime later, Joyce went into the restroom and there was the lady, reading her New Testament.

The girl in the next seat looked frightened. They were on a small commuter plane.

Joyce introduced herself and said, "There's a verse in the Bible about the Lord protecting our going out and coming in. I change it to say 'my going up and my coming down,'" she added, laughing.

"I'm sure glad you're beside me," the girl said.

The flight was tempestuous. Engaging her in conversation to keep her occupied, Joyce learned that the girl grew up just a few miles from York and was traveling home to visit her parents.

When they landed, Joyce pulled out a Bible and read Psalm 121:7–8.

The Lord will preserve thee from all evil: he shall preserve thy soul. The Lord shall preserve thy going out and thy coming in from this time forth, and even for evermore (KJV).

"That is what God's Word has to say about being afraid," she said, giving her the Bible and suggesting she read it, beginning with the Gospel of John.

A young father and his two small sons were flying across the country. Joyce first encountered them in the airport and learned that they had just attended the man's sister's wedding. The father had been an usher and the older child the ring bearer. They had taken the baby to meet his relatives for the first time. The boys' mother hadn't been able to go because of her job. Cups, bottles and stuffed animals peeked from the large pockets in the father's shorts. He carried blankets to soothe the baby and encourage sleep.

When they boarded a connector flight, Joyce's seat was directly across the aisle from the three.

"I'm hoping they'll stay awake here and sleep on the cross-country flight," the father confessed.

As they spoke, Joyce sensed he was a Christian. She offered words of encouragement.

When the plane began to descend, she reached

across the aisle and placed her hand on his arm. Praying quietly, she asked the Lord to give the little ones sleep and to reunite the family safely.

The father thanked her gratefully.

As Joyce recalled these encounters, she reflected again on the importance of parents' prayers for their children, noting the part they played in several of them.

"I just wonder what happened to all those people after that," she says. "Even if they stuck the testament in a drawer, there will be a time when they'll need it and it will be there. My part is to put God's Word in their hands. It's the Holy Spirit's job to do the rest."

*Not real name

CHAPTER SIXTEEN

MALL STORIES

The girl was dressed in black from head to foot. Heavy chains circled her neck and hung from her waist. Tattoos and body piercings completed the picture. It was impossible not to notice her, even in the Friday night mall crowd.

Joyce had gone to a town several hours away from home for a speaking engagement. A friend accompanied her. They arrived the afternoon before and asked the motel manager to recommend eating places. He pointed out several within walking distance of the motel and the mall beyond them. They opted for the mall. The signature restaurant there, however, had a long waiting line, so they decided to try the food court. The girl was on the escalator approaching it.

"That's some mother's daughter," Joyce said to her friend, tears filling her eyes.

As they were scanning the eating opportunities,

the girl crossed in front of Joyce and said, "Excuse me."

They got their food and sat down. The girl and a young man were at a table within their view.

Joyce played with her food. Finally she spoke to her friend.

"Would I embarrass you if I went over to talk with them? I have no idea what I will say, but I just have to go."

Her friend assured her she wouldn't, then quietly prayed for her and watched as she walked to their table, spoke briefly, pulled up a chair and sat down. The conversation seemed to be reciprocal. Then Joyce and the girl arose and hugged and Joyce returned to her table.

"You're not going to believe this," she said, beginning to tell the story.

She had asked the two if she could talk to them a few minutes. When they didn't resist she pulled up the chair and sat down, directing the conversation to the girl.

"You probably don't remember, but you walked in front of me a few moments ago and excused yourself," she said. "I don't want to offend you, but it's obvious that you're making a statement by the way you're dressed. Do you find that people sometimes avoid you because of your appearance?"

The girl acknowledged this was so and Joyce told her she had the opposite reaction.

"I just had to talk to you," she explained. "My name is Joyce."

The girl said she was Susan* and her friend was Brian.* She told Joyce that she was a student at a nearby college and Brian was a graduate in psychology. Brian announced rather proudly that he was moving to California.

Joyce asked if Susan was going along.

"If she does, we'll have one big party," Brian replied.

Then Joyce told Susan she'd like to give her something and reached into her pocket and pulled out a little Bible.

Before she got a chance to offer it, Susan said, "Oh, that's a Gideon Bible. I have one of those."

Somewhat taken aback, Joyce paused.

"You see," the girl went on, "my dad is a minister. He had a church here for many years and then we moved to Florida. We just came back."

As Joyce tried to hide her surprise, Susan named her father's denomination, adding that Joyce probably wasn't familiar with it. Joyce was very familiar with it.

Now kindred spirits, Susan and Joyce went on to discuss a well-known church camp in the area.

"Oh, I love that camp," Susan said. "I was there just last summer."

At that point, Brian stood up, stating that they'd have to leave if they were going to the movies.

Susan agreed and Joyce asked if she could give her a hug.

Neither Joyce nor her friend slept well that night and concurred in the morning that thoughts of Susan and Brian had kept them awake. They had both filled their waking hours with prayer.

Joyce spoke to a large group of ladies that day, setting aside some of what she planned to say to tell them about Susan and Brian. Many ladies agreed to pray for them.

Only eternity will reveal the outcome of that encounter, but the circumstances leading to it could not have been happenstance. Joyce wondered if they were put into place by parents' prayers.

Joyce goes nowhere without praying for divine appointments. She was sure this was one.

Joyce and Morgan had gone to a local mall. They had a rare night to themselves and were in no hurry to go home. They bought pretzels and sat down on a bench.

"My heart felt grieved for all the kids, especially the young girls," Joyce said.

She asked Morgan where he thought their parents were and whether they had any idea what they were doing.

Morgan said he was glad their children were raised.

"But we have grandchildren in this generation," Joyce said. "I feel like crying for all these lost young folks."

She thought about something she had read recently about a light shining brighter in the darkness than in the daylight and mentioned it to Morgan.

Then she prayed, "Dear Lord, Morgan and I are sitting here in this mall. You are sitting here with us.

I feel Your pain. I will not move until You bring someone along that You want me to talk to."

When she looked up, she saw Terri* walking toward them, accompanied by a young man. Terri had lived at The Lighthouse for more than a year. After she left, she had quit coming to church. She looked uncomfortable when she saw Joyce and Morgan.

Joyce greeted her warmly and asked her to introduce her friend. They talked a few minutes, and then Joyce told Terri she'd be looking for her in church the next morning and invited the young man to come along. He said he'd come—sometime.

Watching them walk away, Joyce remembered her prayer. Had this been another divine appointment?

When they first entered the mall, Joyce saw a crowd of people watching a young man in a heavy metal vest. The man was on a dance machine. Later, they passed that way again and saw him still dancing—this time with a girl in eye-catching attire.

After their encounter with Terri, Joyce saw the dancing couple coming toward them. They passed by and entered a small restaurant where they seated themselves and began to play a card game.

"I am going to talk to them," Joyce told Morgan. "I'm curious about what they are doing."

Joyce walked over to the eating establishment and introduced herself.

Looking surprised, they told her their names.

She commented about the dance and how much energy it took to do it.

The man told her he had asthma and his metal vest weighed twenty-five pounds. He said his doctor recommended the exercise.

Reminding him to drink a lot of water and eat well, Joyce went back to Morgan. When he suggested it was time to leave, she asked him to go with her to meet the couple first. There were two other uniquely dressed men there when they reached the table and they chatted with all of them for a while. As they turned to walk away, Jim* (the dancer) thanked Joyce for her interest in them.

"I didn't say anything about the Lord," Joyce said later, "but I may still get a chance. That isn't the first time I saw Jim at that mall. If nothing else, I bridged the generation gap."

Joyce had just dropped off a roll of film at Wal-Mart.

"Lord," she prayed, "I have a whole hour to wait. What would You have me do?"

She decided on a cup of coffee at McDonald's and immediately noticed a woman in a wheelchair. The woman had a toy frog taped to her shoe.

"I like your frog," Joyce said.

"I got it at the fair," the woman replied.

"I love the fair," Joyce volunteered. "I've gone every year since I was five years old."

Joyce asked the woman where she lived and learned she was from a local cerebral palsy group home.

"I come on the bus," she said. "They all think I'm crazy for doing it."

Joyce asked her name and learned it was Elaine.*

"Elaine, do you know Jesus?" Joyce asked.

"Oh, I do," Elaine replied. "That's the only reason I can come to the mall like this."

Joyce reached for a New Testament for Elaine and then decided the print would probably be too small for her. She suggested she give it to her favorite nurse and Elaine put the Testament in the bag attached to her wheelchair.

"Is there anything I can do for you?" Joyce asked.

"Actually, I'm hungry," Elaine replied. "I had to rush so much to get the bus that I missed lunch."

Joyce suddenly remembered she didn't have much money with her, but she and Elaine put together enough for a hot dog, French fries, and a drink and Joyce brought them to the table.

"You're like a nurse," Elaine said.

"I am a nurse," Joyce replied, suggesting they pray together before Elaine ate.

"Oh, thank you," Elaine said. "They don't understand this at the home, but Jesus always takes care of me when I come to the mall."

"There are no coincidences when you know the Lord," Joyce says. "These are the kind of experiences that should be part of our everyday lives. We just need to pray and make ourselves available."

*Not real names

CHAPTER SEVENTEEN

WINTER WONDERLAND

Part I

"**A** long time before we lived here we brought our children to see the Christmas display on Country Club Road," Joyce recalls. "Never in my wildest imagination did I dream that someday those decorations would be in our front yard."

The decorations were originally the property of Dr. Pfaltzgraff, a local dentist. One Christmas, when the York Chamber of Commerce was trying to encourage people to come into the city, they introduced a contest for best decorations. Dr. Pfaltzgraff, who lived on the main street in the city, responded by building a large snowman for his front yard. Each year after that, he added something. By the time the display got too large for the city location, Dr. and Mrs. Pfaltzgraff moved to Country Club Road, across from the house that eventually became The Lighthouse.

"Dr. Pfaltzgraff never had children of his own," Morgan said, "but he loved his little patients. All the toys he put on his decorations were brought in by them."

Morgan calls the structure of the decorations "intriguing."

"They all have leather straps and gears," he explains. "Dr. Pfaltzgraff's philosophy was that they all had to move up, down, and around."

Each year Dr. Pfaltzgraff put the display out right after Thanksgiving and took it in on New Year's Day. One New Year's Day, shortly after Joyce and Morgan moved to Country Club Road, Dr. Pfaltzgraff had a heart attack. His doctor advised him not to put the decorations out after that. When Dr. Pfaltzgraff recovered, Joyce asked him if he had a nativity set they could put in their yard the next year.

"This is just a children's winter wonderland," Dr. Pfaltzgraff replied, "but I'll tell you what. If Morgan would be willing to put the decorations in your yard so that I could sit and watch them, I'd love that."

Morgan gave it some thought, then asked Dr. Pfaltzgraff if he was interested in selling the decorations. The doctor immediately said no, but the next day beckoned Morgan over.

"Polly and I talked about the decorations last night," he said, "and decided we'd sell them to you for the price of the gear boxes."

The two worked out an agreement and the display found a new permanent home.

"After I bought them," Morgan relates, "I checked out how he had everything set up. Then I came home and built a substation from which I can run anything. Each string of lights is on a separate circuit."

"We carted all the decorations across the street and Dr. Pfaltzgraff showed Morgan how to assemble them," Joyce added. "The next two years, he sat on our front porch drinking hot chocolate and giving instructions when Morgan got the decorations out. Mrs. Pfaltzgraff always said if Dr. Pfaltzgraff had a son, he would be like Morgan."

The following spring, Uncle Claude sent Joyce and Morgan's family to Disney World. When they returned, they learned the sad news that Dr. Pfaltzgraff had died while they were gone.

From the beginning, Frosty the Snowman was the main attraction of the display. During the year, Dr. Pfaltzgraff kept Frosty in his basement connected to a light switch. When anyone flipped the switch, Frosty blinked his eyes and waved. Frosty turned fifty in 2002.

"The decorations have definitely become a tradition," Joyce stated. "People start calling in October to ask if we're putting them out."

That, in itself, is no small task. A dolly, pulled by Morgan's tractor, brings Frosty up the inclined driveway from the garage. He is returned the same way. Maintenance at the end of the season is another undertaking. Morgan washes and repairs each piece before carefully returning it to its box.

"When the children were small, decorating the yard was a family affair," Joyce says. "It was a highlight of their lives. Now we turn to our grandchildren for help."

There have only been four years when the decorations didn't come out, including the year Joyce's mother died and another year during an energy crunch.

"People have asked why we don't put a nativity set out," Joyce says. "I would never put a nativity set in among those things. It's a winter wonderland, as Dr. Pfaltzgraff used to say. The decorations are our sanctified bait."

Recalling some of the ways the display has opened doors to share the real meaning of Christmas, she says, "They're an icebreaker. We've always invited people into the yard for a closer look and in earlier years, members of the family were often there to talk with them."

She remembers finding notes in the mailbox from visitors and seeing groups of senior citizens coming by in vans. A friend brought her son to see the display the day before he died; a woman brought her five-year-old niece who was losing her eyesight to cancer. They knocked on the door to say thank you before they left.

After these many years, the decorations have become a point of identification. Often when Joyce and Morgan are introduced, it's with the add-on, "You know, that house on Country Club Road with the Christmas decorations."

Part II

Although you may not find a nativity set in front of The Lighthouse, there's no end to them inside the house. Some are visible year-round; most come out after Thanksgiving.

"Through the years, we have received nativity sets from all over the world," Joyce says. "Getting them out brings back many memories."

The sets also have special meaning for the grandchildren who are there for Christmas.

"I hide the nativities all over the house and have a contest to see who can find the most," Joyce explains.

That's not as easy as it may sound, for the sets come in all forms. There are glass ones, brass ones, wooden ones, and silver ones. One is a puzzle, one a tree ornament. A tiny one is in a bottle and one once appeared in the aquarium. There's a Precious Moments nativity set and a snowman one. A Native American set has buffaloes instead of camels and an Eskimo set has an igloo for the stable. There are two nativity set "nests" (stacked inside each other) from Russia—the tiniest figure on the inside being an angel.

One of the most precious to Joyce is a paper mâche set that survived the flood of 1972. She and Morgan received it the year they were married.

"We lost almost all our Christmas decorations in the flood," Joyce says, "but we revived those pieces and laid them out to dry. All of them except the figure of Jesus dried perfectly. That one is flawed."

"I still put that set on the mantle every year, though," she adds. "It's special to the children because they grew up with it and it reminds me of the price Jesus paid for me."

There's a set from Ecuador—a gift from Maria, a former resident at The Lighthouse—made of flour and painted by hand; several sets from Peru; several sets from Africa—one handmade and painted by African friends; sets from Indonesia, Germany, and Thailand... the list goes on. There are approximately 120 of them.

Picture, if you will, the front door of The Lighthouse opening on Christmas morning and Mark and Miriam's fifteen children bursting in. After hugs and kisses all around, all who are old enough hurry off to find nativity sets.

"They are very orderly," Joyce says. "They don't let on when they see one, they just count it. Of course there's a prize for the winner."

What better memories could children have—a winter wonderland of decorations outside, nativity sets inside, and Jesus at the heart of everything!

CHAPTER EIGHTEEN

COZY COTTAGE

How do you "grandparent" fifteen children in one family from a distance?

This was Joyce and Morgan's dilemma as Mark and Miriam's family continued to grow. Although they were welcomed with open arms when they visited, sleeping accommodations became a problem. They loved having the family visit them, but often wished for more time to talk with individual children and Mark and Miriam. There had to be an answer.

For starters, they parked an RV on the hill behind Mark's farm. Then Mark saw a trailer for sale and called his dad.

Joyce laughs when she remembers the call.

"Mark said he wanted Morgan to come up and look at a trailer which was wheelchair accessible," she says. "When Morgan told me, I wondered if Mark thought we were ready for wheelchairs."

Even though Morgan was preparing to leave for

Haiti, the decision had to be made because the trailer's owner wanted it moved. After a quick trip to look at it, Morgan and Mark discussed the details, the owner having agreed to hold it till they were worked out.

Morgan parked the RV by the road with a "For Sale" sign and sold it in one day—for the amount he needed for the trailer. Then the man he hired to put in a septic system asked if he'd like him to move the trailer to its new spot. He "just happened" to have the equipment to do that as well. So, the transaction was finalized and the trailer was placed where the RV had been.

"The children were so excited," Joyce said.

When Morgan returned from the mission to Haiti, he and Joyce went up to inspect their new home away from home.

One of the first things Joyce noticed was that there was room for a kitchen table—a must in her book. She stocked a closet with puzzles, books, and games, remembering the span of ages and interests. Now the children could come individually or in groups for sleepovers, games, cookie baking, or talks with Grandma and Grandpa.

Morgan's first vision was a deck, which he soon built with the help of several of the boys. A picnic table on the deck increased seating capacity—at least in warm weather. The older boys made a fire circle, collecting stones to surround the campfires over which they would roast hot dogs and marshmallows.

Joyce remembers well the first time she sat on

the deck and watched several of the children walk up the hill. It was like a dream come true.

"We've got to give this place a name," she decided one day. She sent the word through the family, announcing a contest to name the trailer. Forty names were submitted and by popular vote the trailer became "Cozy Cottage." Nine-year-old Esther won a birdhouse for her entry.

"Mother, this is for a season," Joyce recalls Mark saying. She wasn't sure why he said it several times.

One of the most difficult adjustments to caring for Morgan's mother (Chapter 21) has been the lack of freedom to use Cozy Cottage. After several attempts to take Grandma with them, it became apparent it was easier to care for her at home. So for now, trips to the cottage are limited. Occasionally, Mark and Miriam share it with visiting missionaries and from time to time family members use it, but for the most part it sits empty.

"It's for a season," Mark had said.

"There is a time for everything, and a season for every activity under heaven" (Ecclesiastes 3:1).

CHAPTER NINETEEN

MIYUKI

Hello Miyuki,

It's quite late, but before I go to bed, I want to drop you a few lines, mainly to say hello and fill you in on what is happening here at The Lighthouse. We are all looking forward to your arrival. Beth and her little daughters (Amee and Ashley) are still here. We celebrated Ashley's 4th birthday this evening. It was very special. Their time here is passing by very quickly. They will be leaving for their home on Monday, 31st. Amee's school starts on August 1st. We have had a wonderful time and made a lot of special memories.

Our daughter Amy and her family moved into The Lighthouse last week. Their return trip to Africa has been postponed for a few weeks because of the political situation in Côte d'Ivoire. So they will be here when you arrive. August 10th is their 15-year wedding anniversary, so they may take a holiday for a few days and I will be keeping the children. So, the night that Morgan and I come to the airport to pick you up, we will have Abby, age 10 years, Kari, 7 years, and Peter, 3 years, along to greet you.

You will be staying in the basement bedroom until Amy and Steve leave for Africa and after they leave you can move up to Amy's room. However if you like the room downstairs you are welcome to stay there.

On Sunday, our son Mark and wife Miriam and all 13* of their children will be here. They are coming to go to church with us. Our son-in-law Steve will be speaking and sharing some concerns of his heart with our church friends and Amy will be singing. Our oldest daughter Shonna will also be there. After church, they will all be here for lunch. We are having a birthday party for Ben, who will be 15 years old. He is Mark's 2nd son.

I am so excited, Miyuki, for you to meet all of my family members.

On August 1st, Junko and her son will be arriving from Japan. We haven't seen her for 15 years. I am happy that you two will meet. Maybe you will be able to continue a friendship. She is a wonderful person and I think you are also.

Well, Miyuki, it's past my bedtime so I will sign off for now and say "goodnight."

Warmly,

Joyce.

That was the last e-mail Miyuki Omori received from Joyce before arriving in York in July of 2001.

Joyce says she spent a lot of time writing to Miyuki that summer so that she wouldn't be overwhelmed by the people and activity at The Lighthouse.

"I thought if I used names in my letters, it would be easier for her to put names and faces together when she got here," she explains.

Abby, Kari, and Peter did go along to the airport and were standing with Joyce and Morgan, holding a "Welcome Miyuki" sign when she arrived. Miyuki kept the sign in her room for a long time.

"I had studied about the U.S., so I didn't have big shock," Miyuki says of their airport meeting. "I did think American people were taller than me but Joyce was shorter."

Because she knew about the children, Miyuki brought Japanese toys with her. They helped with the transition that first evening. At a picnic at Shonna's the next night, three-year-old Peter came to the rescue. While the adults talked after the meal, he and Miyuki wrestled and played together.

Miyuki says that when she graduated from high school in Japan, she learned that the new school she had attended did not have the reputation of more established schools. Thus, she needed a higher GPA for acceptance at a university. She decided to "take the easy way" and enrolled at a vocational school to learn English.

"I didn't study," she says, "but I received (the equivalent of) an associate degree and got a job."

Several jobs and a few years later, Miyuki came

to regret her lack of ambition and started studying English "as a hobby."

"Then I thought if I could go to a university in the U.S., I would take English as a second language."

She applied to several, was accepted at three and chose York College. In correspondence with the registrar, she learned that only people under 25 could live on campus, so she asked for help in finding housing. Someone suggested The Lighthouse and arrangements were soon made.

Having been impressed with Miyuki's letters (prior to her arrival), Joyce didn't expect communication problems. However, what she didn't know was that the letters were written with the help of a dictionary. Verbal communication was a different matter.

"It took a year," Joyce said. "We struggled with both language and cultural differences."

Miyuki, too, remembers the difficulties.

"I think I didn't understand English very well. Listening was OK but reading (textbooks) was difficult.

"The first year I didn't have a close friend," she continued. "When I was a sophomore, I met two girls from InterVarsity Christian Fellowship at the International Student's Club. We would talk when I would see them, but I wasn't Christian. I didn't believe anything."

Miyuki explained that eight percent of the people in her country have no religion and those who do are thought to need help (counseling).

"In my twenties, I had some New Age ideas and I did believe in reincarnation. I was reading many business books which told me if I worked hard, I can do anything. I bought into that. I didn't know anything about Jesus and never met a Christian in Japan," she added.

Despite her background, Miyuki agreed to go to church with Morgan and Joyce the first Sunday.

Joyce remembers a conversation between Miyuki and Amy in the car on the short drive there.

"What is church and what do you do at church?" Miyuki asked.

"We read the Bible and pray and get together with other Christians," Amy replied.

As they neared the building, Joyce heard Amy saying, "When mother came to the airport to pick you up, you didn't know her but you had read her e-mails. That's why we read the Bible—to get to know God."

That was just the first of many conversations about spiritual matters. Miyuki joined a small group to learn more about Christianity but was uncomfortable when people talked about personal matters.

"I thought it was weird," she says.

But she continued to attend a college students' group.

"I didn't understand what they were talking about," she admits.

Once, Miyuki told Joyce that she wasn't going to become a Christian until she understood the whole

Bible. "Well, Miyuki," Joyce replied, "it may never happen then."

Miyuki credits Joyce and Morgan's attitude and Lisa, one of the girls from InterVarsity, with helping her to understand Christianity.

"Lisa was very helpful. We became close friends. She told me about God's love. I started to understand."

"After that," she continued, "I was able to understand what Joyce and Morgan were doing—helping people."

Miyuki began attending InterVarsity meetings with regularity.

"People were very nice. I felt very comfortable. Then I decided to believe Jesus Christ," she states. "It was a conscious decision that I made by myself."

The Bible was Miyuki's next concern.

"I didn't understand the Bible," she says. "I became dependent on my friends."

Concerning that time in Miyuki's life, Joyce cites part of Matthew 7:7, *Seek and you will find."*

"If anyone sought the Lord, Miyuki did," she says. "She spent a lot of time reading the Word."

A friend from Miyuki's small group remembers her English/Japanese Bible, noting that the columns were side by side. "She would read one and then the other," she says. "And questions," she adds, "Miyuki asked questions, questions, questions."

Miyuki recalls a time at the end of her junior year when a Jewish student talked about joining school activities.

"Up to then, I went to InterVarsity and International Club, but was very passive. I realized I needed to be active."

Soon, Miyuki was nominated for vice president of the International Club and became involved in the student senate.

"I wanted to be representative of minority students," she said.

Miyuki wrote an article about campus littering that led to an invitation to become a staff writer for the college newsletter. Because she worked on the ground crew at the college, she wrote an article about her job to "help people appreciate what people who work as janitors do." She also interviewed campus professors for feature articles.

Miyuki is very aware of how she has changed since she came to America.

"My thinking has changed," she states. "I believe I am born again. I take life more seriously. I used to be scared of many things—like ghosts. Now I am not afraid. I only fear (reverence) God."

Although The Lighthouse had much to do with Miyuki's transition, both she and Joyce admit they had to work at their relationship.

"It took a year before I realized that when she said yes, she meant no," Joyce said.

"Before I became a Christian, Joyce and I had some arguments and she asked me to leave," Miyuki remembers. "After I became a Christian, I understood Joyce and Morgan more than before. We are much more comfortable with each other."

Joyce recalls that time. She had become discouraged about communication with Miyuki and with her refusal to embrace the claims of Christ. Finally, she summoned her courage and suggested that she find another place to live for the next school year.

Immediately, Miyuki informed her that two of her Japanese friends had asked her to share an apartment with them. Just as Joyce was about to offer a sigh of relief, Miyuki added, "But I said no. If I live with them I will not learn about Christianity and here I can learn about Christianity."

That settled the matter and Miyuki stayed.

Reflecting, Miyuki shared the following observations about her years at The Lighthouse:

I'm very lucky to be here. Now I understand what they are doing. It's very helpful.

Reading the Bible—talking about God. It never happened (to me) before.

In Japan, we just eat and not thank anybody. Here we pray before we eat. Now, when I go to a Japanese friend's house that is not Christian, that's very different. Even though she's a very kind and nice person, I feel something's missing.

If people grew up in Christian families, it's not very special (to them), but to me it's very special. Atmosphere here is very different from non-believers.

They have many Christian friends that visit here. If I see Christian friends, I feel love and affection, but when I see non-believers, even though they are nice people, I don't feel that.

During her senior year in college, Miyuki decided to be baptized. Joyce and Morgan and many of her Christian friends joyfully witnessed the occasion. On the day she graduated from York College, many came to an open house at The Lighthouse to celebrate her achievement and rejoice in what God had done in her life.

As a shy freshman, Miyuki Omori didn't believe anything, had trouble communicating, couldn't read her textbooks, and lacked friends. As a senior, she was confident, had many friends, was a student leader, and a believer in the Lord Jesus Christ. When she asked Joyce and Morgan if she could stay at The Lighthouse one more year, they readily agreed. Although it hadn't occurred overnight, Miyuki had become part of the family and it would be hard to see her go.

*Two children have been added to Mark's family since Miyuki arrived in America.

CHAPTER TWENTY

ABDUCTION

J oyce wasn't home when the phone rang on August 7, 2001. Morgan answered and was pleasantly surprised to hear Amy's voice. After a brief greeting, Amy asked if her mother was there. Morgan said she wasn't. Then Amy said she wanted to talk to both of them and would like them to call back as soon as her mother returned.

Although this was a bit unusual, Morgan wasn't concerned. When Joyce arrived and he told her, she recalled that Steve had been ill the last time she had talked to Amy. Perhaps he had gotten worse—possibly had malaria.

She also thought about the political situation in Bouake, which had been tense for more than a year and had delayed Amy and Steve's return from their last home assignment.

Joyce quickly placed the call to Africa while Morgan waited on another phone. Nothing they had imagined prepared them for what they heard. Amy's words ran together.

"I'm all right... I wanted you to hear it from me... you'll be getting e-mails... there will be all sorts of rumors... I'm all right."

Afterwards, Morgan and Joyce struggled to put it together.

Steve and another missionary, who was new to the field, had gone to a meeting. Amy knew that the missionary's wife was homesick and a bit discouraged, so she suggested they meet at a Lebanese restaurant for *schwarmas*, (goat meat wrapped in grape leaves). Kari was visiting a friend. Abby and Peter went with Amy, the missionary, and her two children.

While they were eating, five men entered the restaurant. Abby was the first to see a gun. As she started to inform her mother, the men told the party to get down on the floor. Taking their pocketbooks and jewelry, they turned to leave, then looked at Amy and said, "You're coming with us." To the horror of her children and the others, Amy was taken from the restaurant, a gun in her back.

Outside, she was forced into a car and, at gunpoint, ordered to take the bandits to a place where they could get more money. They threatened to defile her and even to take her life.

The only place Amy could think of was the guesthouse which was also their mission office. As they drove there, the men slapped her and hit her with the butts of their guns. When they arrived at the guest house, the kidnappers pummeled the husband

and wife who were in charge. The husband had no choice but to open the safe and give them the mission's money.

Having gotten what they wanted, the party left quickly—still with Amy in tow.

They drove around for a short period of time, then for no apparent reason, stopped and released her in a dark, deserted neighborhood, one of the men asking her to give him a kiss on the cheek as they departed.

Exhausted and disoriented, Amy wandered around crying for help. Miraculously, two African men appeared out of the darkness.

"We are Christians. How can we help you?" they asked.

As soon as they could comprehend what she was telling them, they walked her to a nearby pastor's house. He took her back to the guesthouse, where Steve and the children had gone to await information.

Joyce and Morgan were amazed at the calmness with which Amy told her story. She kept reassuring them that she was safe. Her courage softened the horror of the ordeal for them. But, finally, her voice broke and—more than 5,000 miles apart—the three cried together.

"We felt so sad, so helpless," Joyce said later.

"We wanted to hold her in our arms and tell her it was going to be all right, but we couldn't."

After Joyce and Morgan hung up, they prayed. Then they called the rest of the family and prayer partners near and far. But they still felt that awful distance separating them from their daughter. They were unable to reach across it. Amy was in West Africa and they were in Pennsylvania. How could they bridge that gap?

It was then that Morgan remembered an experience he'd had several weeks earlier.

"I was talking to the Lord about all of our children, but especially about Amy, and I was just overwhelmed," he recalled. "I told God that, as Amy's father, I felt I had to protect her."

Choking back tears, he continued.

"The Holy Spirit spoke to me. He told me it was impossible for me to protect her, but that her heavenly Father was caring for her and I needed to release her to His loving care."

Now, on this day, when Morgan told Joyce of that experience, they did something they had first done long ago – and have done since—they gave their daughter back to God.

"When we did that," Joyce recalled, "this overwhelming peace came. It was indescribable."

That same peace met them at the gap which they could not physically cross to reach Amy. They would need to return to it many times in the ensuing weeks, for Amy's abductors remained at large and she had eye-to-eye contact with them on three occasions. Finally, the threat of further violence made it necessary for Amy and Steve to leave their beloved Bouake and relocate to Abidjan, Côte d'Ivoire, 220 kilometers to the south. After a short time there, political unrest forced them, along with other American missionaries, out of Côte d'Ivoire. Amy and Steve found themselves waiting on God for their next assignment. It turned out to be Burkina Faso.

Amidst all the turmoil surrounding Amy's ordeal, there were many evidences of God's intervention. Obviously, her unexplained release and the appearance of the two African Christians were God-things.

None, however, was more poignant than the story of some African women whom Amy had mentored. They were together when they received word of her abduction and immediately began to pray.

Later they told her, "You taught us how to pray and we did. We prayed in every language we knew. We even tried praying in English. Now we *know* God answers prayer."

CHAPTER TWENTY-ONE

GRANDMA HELEN

J oyce says she tries not to anticipate things too much. That way she doesn't set herself up for disappointment.

But she did look forward to the month of June 2002. Amy, Steve, Abby, Kari, and Peter were coming home from Africa on a premature furlough because of Amy's abduction; Jonas, Beth, Amee, and Ashley were flying in from Colorado; Shonna had planned a trip to the seashore for everyone, and Mark and Miriam were making preparations for a big weekend at the farm.

Joyce cooked and cleaned for most of the month of May. The freezer was full because she didn't want to spend all her time in the kitchen when everyone was home. She wanted to be able to enjoy her family.

Morgan's mother lived not far from Joyce and Morgan. Having turned ninety-two on her last birthday, she was still independent, despite showing signs of dementia. Morgan stopped often; Joyce took food, and neighbors kept a close eye on her.

But Joyce and Morgan knew the day was approaching when she would come to live with them. They had discussed it and agreed that's what they'd do—when the time came.

The time came one morning in June 2002. Amy and Steve had arrived but were visiting Steve's mother and sisters. Beth's family had not yet come. Joyce was dressing for work and Morgan was getting ready to pick up his mother for her weekly hair appointment. The phone rang. It was one of Helen's neighbors calling to alert them to some issues concerning her safety. Joyce took the call and handed the phone to Morgan.

"Today is D-Day," Morgan said decisively when he hung up.

"I didn't think he was serious," Joyce recalled later.

But when she came home from work, Helen was there.

Morgan filled her in. He had gone to the house and told his mother he was taking her to have her hair done after which she was coming to live with them. She accepted it without question.

Acceptance did not come as easily to Joyce. Suddenly, sleeping accommodations for the family reunion had to be rearranged and preparations for the shore trip had to be expanded to include Grandma. They needed to move essentials from her house to theirs and establish a new daily routine.

A few days later, the children and grandchildren arrived. Joyce's long experience in being flexible had prepared her well and she rose to the occasion.

"They thought it was wonderful to have Grandma here during their visit," Joyce recalled.

All too soon the vacations came to an end. Beth's family returned to Colorado and Amy and Steve went back to Africa. Helen was perfectly content, often saying, "We sure have a nice place. How long have we lived here now?"

Morgan participated in his mother's care and Joyce continued to work her regular schedule. For a while, life wasn't too different.

Then the political situation in Côte d'Ivoire took a turn for the worse, and Amy and Steve were forced out—with no options but to come home again.

Joyce and Morgan turned the lower level of the house over to them and the place took on the busyness of two families, plus Grandma. Seth (Mark's oldest) and Miyuki were also still there. The total count was ten, across four generations.

Amy took a teaching job at the local Christian school and enrolled the children there. Joyce loved serving her family—packing sandwiches, attending school events, and hearing about her grandchildren's days. But the demands of caring for Helen were becoming greater.

Joyce had committed herself to speak at a women's retreat at Beth's church in Colorado that fall. The theme was *Soaring to New Heights—All Ages, All Stages.*

"Suddenly, I was really in conflict," she says. "I

wasn't soaring. I wanted to back out. I knew I couldn't speak without victory over the situation at home.

"I cried out to the Lord," she confessed. "I prayed, *'Search me, O God, and know my heart: try me and know my thoughts'* (Psalm 139:23). I wanted to really love Helen and I wanted to be a good example to my children and grandchildren."

As Joyce opened herself to the Lord, He walked her back through the years. Painfully, she acknowledged that her relationship with Helen had never been easy. Now she was being asked to sacrificially care for her. The struggle was difficult, but God had been faithful during the years she had cared for Uncle Claude and in her heart she knew that He was adequate for this.

"He showed me simple things like giving Helen a hug every day and telling her I loved her," she remembers. "Sometimes she would respond and say, 'You're so good to me.'"

Finally, by the time she left to lead the retreat, Joyce was walking in victory once again, and God used her struggles to touch the lives of many women.

After the retreat, a missionary couple who had rented Helen's house for a brief time moved out, and Amy and Steve decided to live there for the rest of their furlough. Amy enjoyed fixing up the place that had such good memories, and Joyce was still able to be in daily contact with the children.

Then the year ended, and Amy's family left for Burkina Faso. Because of all that had transpired, it was harder to say goodbye this time, and once they were gone, Joyce came face-to-face with the fact that her primary role was now that of caregiver.

"The Lord was still teaching me lessons," she says, "and I wanted to learn them. I didn't want my attitude to affect my marriage or my relationship with my heavenly Father."

So, again, she humbled herself and asked God to help her care for Helen with His love. She cut back on her work hours and concentrated on developing an attitude of gratitude. She began to see the positive aspects of what they were doing, and she praised the Lord for Morgan's support and involvement.

"We've developed the most wonderful teamwork," she once said. "It takes both of us to do this well."

Lest other caregivers should think that she never struggled again, Joyce still acknowledges that this assignment from the Lord was her most difficult.

Agreeing, Shonna said, "The hardest thing I've seen Mother do is take Grandma into her home."

"Anybody who has been a caregiver will know," Joyce added.

In time, Joyce had the joy of hearing each of her children express appreciation for what she was doing for Grandma, and she began to feel peace about being obedient to what God had asked of her. One morning, she turned on the radio just as Dr. Woodrow Kroll was speaking to caregivers.

"Just remember," she heard him say, 'Jesus is the caregiver to the caregiver.'"

"That was like a gift to me," she says. "It was a divine appointment."

And Grandma Helen, who was known for her loud "amens" when she attended church services, still says, "We sure have a nice place. How long have we lived here now?"

CHAPTER TWENTY-TWO

MAKING MEMORIES

There were not many days left of their time together. They had returned from the seashore where they had made lots of good memories.

When Joyce got up early Sunday morning, she surveyed the remains of a pizza party the night before. She had been so tired after a reunion with her brothers' and sisters' families the day before that she had gone to bed early. She was glad that Amy and Beth's families had continued to enjoy each other's company.

Now she had a job to do. In the quiet of the sleeping household, she prepared the food for another day. They were all going to Mark and Miriam's.

Mark had put up a big tent. After excited greetings, they gathered there for worship. There were thirty of them. Amy played guitar; Mark spoke about knowing God.

"It was really a great family time," Joyce wrote later.

Following a photo session, lunch was served—then a cake to celebrate Mark's birthday. Grandma Helen was part of all the festivities.

That evening Shonna, Beth, Jonas, Amee, and Ashley left to spend the night at Shonna's; Amy, Steve and Peter returned to The Lighthouse and Morgan, Joyce, Grandma, Kari and Esther went to Cozy Cottage. Abby stayed at Mark and Miriam's.

When the last rays of sunshine had disappeared, Mark's boys arrived at the cottage and built a large campfire. It didn't take long to find hot dogs and marshmallows to roast.

"There was a big, full moon," Joyce recalled. "It was a beautiful night."

Early the next morning, Miriam took Moriah to a nearby hospital to have his tonsils and adenoids removed.

As prearranged, all the remaining grandchildren came to Cozy Cottage for a breakfast of cereal, milk, orange juice, and blueberry muffins. It was a happy time—until Morgan developed a rapid heartbeat. Joyce called the children together and they all laid their hands on him and prayed; then she suggested they also pray for Moriah. Later, they learned that, at that very time, Moriah had also developed a rapid heartbeat and was being transported by ambulance to a medical center where he and his mother spent the next few days.

After some rest, Morgan's heart rate improved and all those who had stayed at the farm prepared to return to York.

"It was so emotional," Joyce said. "The cousins were all crying and saying, 'We'll see you in two years.' It was almost more than I could bear."

The next few days at The Lighthouse were filled with cookouts, swimming, visitors, and conversations. At one point Joyce wrote, "Everyone is in bed except Jonas and Steve, and they are in the living room having a good talk about things of the Lord. It is so neat to hear them. They both have such interesting lives (and wives!)."

"Making memories" is one of Joyce's favorite expressions—and activities. She not only seizes every opportunity to do so, she records each occasion. She always has a disposable camera in her pocketbook and her journals are close at hand. Despite her busy days, she finds time to chronicle each happening—adding clippings, programs, pictures, and comments. In the quiet moments when she's missing her family, she pours a cup of coffee, settles into the chair beside the fireplace—or on the swing by the pool— and reminisces. Sometimes she's overcome with nostalgia, but only for a brief period. Then she praises God for all her dear ones and, once again, places them in His hands.

CHAPTER TWENTY-THREE

JEREMIAH 33:3

"It was the most memorable day…" Joyce said.
Many of Joyce's days are most memorable.

She remembers the February morning in 1970 when she awoke at 3:00 a.m. with Jeremiah 33:3 on her mind "like a neon sign."

"I didn't know much about the Old Testament then, so I got my Bible and read, *'Call unto me and I will answer thee, and show thee great and mighty things, which thou knowest not'* (KJV)."

At that moment, she sat on the edge of her bed and wept, for she felt that the "great and mighty thing" would be Claude's salvation.

Now, thirty-three years later, Joyce was on her way to her job at the doctor's office and the radio announcer was calling Christians to stand on Jeremiah 33:3 that day, March 3, 2003 (3-3-03).

"Lord, I promise to share Jeremiah 33:3 with

everybody I come in contact with today," she prayed.

Throughout the day, Joyce's employer saw thirty patients. Joyce shared Jeremiah 33:3 with every one of them. Later, at a staff luncheon, she shared it with her co-workers, the waiter, and the lady at the front desk. Then, at 3:03 that afternoon, she asked available staff members to join her in prayer just as the radio announcer had suggested.

Hilda* was one of their patients. Having come to America from another country, she was burdened with many problems. When she poured them out, Joyce put her arms around her, shared Jeremiah 33:3 and prayed for her. Hilda told her no one had ever done that before.

Jeremy* was another patient. Several years earlier during an office visit, Joyce had led him in a prayer asking Christ to come into his life. This day, he had his Bible with him and was trying to read Psalm 27.

"That's one of my favorite psalms," Joyce told him as she put a thermometer in his mouth. Taking the Bible, she read it to him and then shared Jeremiah 33:3. Jeremy's wife thanked her.

Reactions from other patients were mixed. Some didn't appear interested, but Joyce was faithful to her promise. One man suggested that she should play the lottery using 3-3-03.

Joyce's final audience at the end of the day was her family gathered around the dinner table. That night it consisted of the four generations: Grandma,

Morgan and Joyce, Steve and Amy and grandchildren Seth, Abby, Kari, and Peter. Miyuki was also there.

Nobody knows Joyce better than her family. As they listened to her story, they shared her excitement and prayed for results in the lives of those who had heard God's Word that day. They all agreed it was indeed a "most memorable day."

*Not real name

CHAPTER TWENTY-FOUR

PEOPLE TALES AND PUPPY SALES

Part I

Many years ago, Joyce heard a speaker talk about the prayer of Jabez.* Afterwards, she wrote in the margin of her Bible, "O Lord, enlarge my tent."

Looking back, she's convinced that's exactly what God did.

The winter after Grandma came to live at The Lighthouse, Joyce and Morgan discussed the fact that they would not be able to take a summer vacation.

Soon afterwards a neighbor, whose house bordered their property, called and asked them to join him and his wife for dinner at a local restaurant. He said he needed to talk to them.

Over the meal, he made his request. He was taking a sabbatical from his teaching job at York College, and he and his wife were going to Europe for seven months. They had arranged to exchange houses with several European families, and they needed an overseer for their property. They envisioned some pick-up and delivery to bus stations and airports, as well as minor maintenance and a check of the house between guests. They had taken great pains to assure that the visiting families could be independent. When Joyce and Morgan agreed to accept the responsibility, they had no idea of the adventure that lay ahead.

The first family came from France, arriving at midnight during a late winter snowstorm. They went to the wrong house, and the puzzled homeowner called and asked Joyce and Morgan if they were expecting guests who didn't speak English. Joyce and Morgan got up and hurried off to greet the mother, father, son, and two daughters. The three siblings loved the snow.

During the French family's stay, they had dinner at The Lighthouse several times, the girls challenged Seth and Miyuki to Scrabble and made French pancakes for them, and the whole family attended church with Joyce and Morgan, responding enthusiastically to the service. In a book at their host home designed for notes to succeeding families, they wrote, "If the Ilgenfritzes invite you to their church, be sure to go."

When the family left to go back to France, they

took French Bibles with them, gifts from Joyce and Morgan.

The next visitors were a couple from England who lived in France. Joyce and Von, the wife, enjoyed each other immensely and Von put her interior decorating skills to work helping Joyce refurbish a room. When Jon and Von left, Joyce gave Von a package of seeds to plant in her English garden as a reminder of their friendship.

Also from France, the next family arrived during the Easter season. They attended the Easter service with Joyce and Morgan and told the pastor afterwards that they had never seen such joy in a church. Later that day, they joined Joyce and Morgan's family for Easter dinner.

Chris was a young policeman from England. He was a free spirit who popped in and out without warning. He was so tall that on one quick visit, he cleaned Joyce's ceiling fan without a ladder. Despite his height, however, he broke the gate between The Lighthouse and the guesthouse when he tried jumping it and failed. Morgan later installed a new one which became known as "Chris's Gate." When Chris returned to England, Joyce and Morgan received this e-mail:

Just a quick note to say I'm home (sadly) but mainly to ask you to nip round and take some tomatoes out of the fridge. I had a sudden flashback and realized I had forgotten to eat them before I left.

Thanks a lot. By the way, you are amongst the few people I have ever met for whom everyone has a good word. Chris

Holding placards, Joyce and Morgan met the next French family at the bus station, taking them to The Lighthouse for iced tea on the way to their vacation residence. Amy, Steve, and the children were home on furlough and five-year-old Peter greeted them in French and told them his name was Pierre.

"Pierre" was about to leave to perform in a children's program at church and Joyce asked the family if they'd like to go along. They accepted the invitation, and had a long talk with the pastor after the program. The teenage daughter and son told Joyce later that it was the first time they had been in a church.

Picnics at The Lighthouse punctuated this family's visit—one with a group of French foreign exchange students who were visiting York. The day after the picnic, Joyce and the French family joined the students and their sponsors on a trip to Washington D.C.

Amy served as interpreter as she, Abby, Kari, and Peter enjoyed activities with the last family. Several members of this family read the first book about The Lighthouse. Later, they admitted they couldn't understand why Joyce and Morgan do the things they do.

Throughout the summer ministry, Joyce and

Morgan shared New Testaments with all the visiting families, often underlining salvation passages.

"God is so good," Joyce reflected. "He knew we couldn't go to faraway places, so He brought the faraway places to us. It was a wonderful summer."

*1 Chronicles 4:10

Part II

When Morgan learned of Seth's desire to become a doctor, he came up with an idea.

"Why don't you breed your golden retriever to get money for college?" he suggested.

It was another open door to adventure. Little did Morgan suspect that he would become chief marketer of golden retriever puppies, answering the inquiries of people who called or knocked on the door.

Each time a litter of puppies is born, a sign goes up in the front yard at The Lighthouse. When the puppies are old enough, Seth brings them from the farm to a pen in the backyard and the transactions take place. It's just one more opportunity to meet people from all walks of life.

Sue was one of those persons. She drove by The Lighthouse regularly and had enjoyed the Christmas decorations for years. In fact, she had been concerned the previous Christmas when they didn't appear and wondered if someone in the family had died.

When she saw the sign, she turned around and drove past it again. She already had a golden retriever but thought she might enjoy a companion. Finally, she parked the car and went to the door, apologizing profusely for stopping at lunchtime.

Joyce invited her in and explained that the puppies were still at her son's house, a couple hours away.

"Is there any way I could see them?" Sue implored.

Seeing an opportunity for a visit with her grand-children, Joyce inquired about Sue's schedule the following week. A day was chosen and the two ladies journeyed to Mark and Miriam's, using the time in the car and over lunch to get acquainted.

When they reached their destination, Joyce played with her grandchildren while Sue got down on the floor with the puppies. By the time they left, Sue had made her choice but had to wait until the puppy was ready to leave her mother.

On the trip home, Joyce asked Sue if she had a church home. Sue admitted to having become care-less about church attendance, and Joyce suggested she join her and Morgan the following Sunday. Sue accepted the invitation, but when she arrived and saw Joyce and Morgan in one of the front pews, she almost left.

"I always sat in the back," she explained.

Mustering her courage, however, she went to the front of the church, slipped in beside them and became engrossed in the service.

Later she asked, "Did you tell your pastor I was coming?"

When Joyce said no, Sue commented that it

seemed he was speaking right to her.

"In fact," she said, "once when I looked at the notes on the overhead screen to try to understand something, he said 'You don't have to look at the PowerPoint, because this isn't there. I just wanted to explain it further.'"

Sue came back that evening to a women's meeting and continued attending Sunday services. After a while, Joyce invited her to dinner. She chose St. Patrick's Day and also asked several others to come.

"Be there at four," she told Sue. "I want to share something with you before we eat."

When the other guests arrived, Miyuki met them at the door, saying quietly, "Come in and sit down. Joyce is talking to someone in the kitchen."

Soon, everyone was called to the dining room and dinner was served. During the meal, Joyce asked Seth and Gideon, a houseguest from Ethiopia, to share the most interesting thing that had happened to them that day. Then she turned to Sue.

"Well, this is my spiritual birthday," Sue said, as cheers erupted from the group.

Part III

For years, Joyce has taught a monthly Bible study at an apartment house near the doctor's office where she works. She loves the ladies who attend and they love her in return. She always takes a "bag of tricks" with her and they look forward to what she has for them each month.

One of Joyce's favorite stories to tell on herself

happened when she first started to teach the group. She was anxious to learn the ladies' names, so as they introduced themselves, she tried to make an association with each one. One lady's name was Blender, so she pictured a kitchen appliance.

When she went back for the second session, Joyce proudly used their names as she greeted each one. When she came to Blender, she said, "Well, hello, Mixer. How are you today?"

Everyone had a good laugh about Joyce's mistake and the ladies have never let her forget it.

Morgan loves to laugh and his laughter is infectious. Recently he told a Sunday school class, "It's so important to laugh together. Joyce and I have laughed more in the last year than we ever did before."

Joyce recalls a recent phone call from one of her sisters.

"Put Morgan on," she said. "I'm feeling down and I want to hear him laugh.

"The Bible says, '*A cheerful heart is good medicine,*'" (Proverbs 17:22) Joyce states. "We all need to laugh more."

CHAPTER TWENTY-FIVE

MORE DIVINE APPOINTMENTS

Part I

Joyce had gone to the dollar store. As she browsed the aisles, she heard children's voices.

"Do you have any flowers?" one asked.

"Yes, we have artificial flowers at the back of the store," a clerk answered.

"No, we want real flowers. Our grandmother gave us money to buy flowers for our mother. She's really sad because our dad's in jail."

Sensing that this was a divine appointment, Joyce walked toward the voices. The boys were obviously brothers, probably of Spanish descent, about eight and ten years old. She learned later that they had walked to the small strip mall from their grandmother's nearby house.

"We don't have fresh flowers," the clerk was telling them, "but maybe the grocery store up on the end does."

The boys hurried off.

Joyce finished her shopping and walked to the grocery store. The boys were just coming out, empty-handed.

"Didn't you find any flowers?" she asked them.

"No, they just have the big pots," one answered.

"I'll tell you what," Joyce said. "I have some beautiful flowers in my yard, (Morgan's prize dahlias). I live near here. Come along with me and I'll fix a bouquet of flowers for your mother."

Without hesitation, the boys crawled into Joyce's van and she took them to The Lighthouse. While they wandered through the yard, she looked for Morgan. When she couldn't find him, she dialed his cell phone. He answered quickly and she asked, "Where are you?"

"I'm working in the (empty) pool," he answered, "and there are two pairs of eyes looking down at me. What's going on?"

"That's what I wanted to tell you about," Joyce replied, laughing.

The boys watched as Joyce fixed the flowers.

"You must be rich," one of them said, looking around the yard.

"God gave us this place," Joyce explained, "and

we use it for Him."

Then she told them that Jesus loved them and cared about their family and that He could forgive whatever their father had done to put him in prison. She gave them each a New Testament, put them back in the van, and took them to the street where their grandmother lived. Before they got out, she got their grandmother's name and phone number.

Later that evening, Joyce called the number and introduced herself. After the grandmother thanked her for her kindness, she asked her to give the boys a message from her.

"Please tell them," she said, "that they are to never, ever go anywhere again with someone they don't know. I happened to be OK, but they have no way of knowing who is and who isn't and they should never take that chance again."

The grandmother agreed and chatted some more. Finally she said, "I'd like to meet you someday. Would that be possible?" Joyce assured her it would and hung up, convinced this wasn't the end of the story.

Part II

Joyce, Morgan, Beth, Jonas, Amee, and Ashley had just arrived in North Carolina for a shared vacation. Unpacking quickly, they hurried to the beach to take a walk. It was almost deserted except for several people walking toward them. As the two groups met, they stopped to talk.

In a short time, it was revealed that the other family had come to the beach to help the mother heal from an accident which had almost taken her life. Soon, both families came to realize they shared a common faith in Christ. When they were about to part, Joyce suggested they pray; they linked arms, thanking God for sparing the young mother's life and asking Him to complete His healing work in her body.

As Joyce's family continued their walk down the beach, Joyce explained to her granddaughters that they had just witnessed a divine appointment.

Part III

Joyce, Morgan, Beth, Amee, and Ashley were on their way home from the vacation in North Carolina, having left Jonas at an airport to fly to a speaking engagement. Tired and hungry after a number of hours on the road, they stopped at a fast food restaurant. It was crowded and they got the last available table.

Suddenly, Joyce wasn't hungry any longer. She ordered yogurt, then decided that the pretzels in the van might taste good with it. That seemed strange to her because she had been snacking on pretzels all morning.

She asked Morgan for his keys. Looking puzzled, he handed them to her. As she walked to the van she saw a man standing by the car parked next to it.

She smiled and said hello and he responded,

adding that it was too crowded in the restaurant for him. He said his family was still eating and he had decided he needed some fresh air. He told her he was from Nigeria.

"At once, I recognized it was a divine appointment," Joyce said, "and I just let the Lord take it from there."

Fifteen minutes later the two returned to the restaurant. Joyce introduced the man to her family and he introduced all of them to his wife and sons. They exchanged e-mail addresses and Joyce gave them a New Testament.

Later that day, she received this e-mail message:

Greetings to you in the exalted name of our Lord and Savior Jesus Christ. I give all glory to God for bringing us together yesterday at McDonald's Restaurant. As we both said, it was a divine connection by God. I thank you for your openness and your love towards me and my family. I also appreciate your husband's love shown toward me and my family. I will keep you in my daily memory and this New Testament and Psalms is a point of contact between your family and mine. I will be applying to York Hospital in September 2004 to the Department of Internal Medicine and/Family Medicine. I will keep you posted. Greetings to your missionary daughter in Burkina Faso when she calls. I hope your journey to York, PA was happy. Remain blessed in the Lord. Sincerely, Dr. John Smith*

"Isn't God good how HE goes before and directs

our path?" Joyce wrote later. "When I talked to that man, I had no idea he was a doctor and was applying to York Hospital."

"Morgan was so dear," she continued. "He saw me from the window and knew God was at work and just continued on with his lunch."

*Not real name

Part IV

It had already been a full day—caring for Grandma, attending a Gideon event, and planting flowers. Morgan had gone to get a truckload of bread for the emus at Mark's farm. Joyce was cleaning out the refrigerator when she came across a bowl of blueberries. She turned to her Amish cookbook, found a recipe for Blueberry Buckle, stirred one together and put it in the oven. She was upstairs with Grandma when Miyuki came up and said there was a man downstairs.

She hurried down and saw him standing by the pool. Although he had his back to her, was many pounds heavier and it was years since she had seen him, she recognized him. He was a former college student from Honduras who had been involved with the International Club and had often visited The Lighthouse.

"Eric," she said. "Eric!"

He turned around, surprised to be remembered, then ran to her, embracing her in a hug.

Morgan was surprised to see Eric when he returned home. As the three of them and Miyuki sat down to enjoy the warm Blueberry Buckle, Joyce prayed, thanking the Lord for bringing Eric to visit. She noticed that he had tears in his eyes when he looked up.

"That's when I knew this was a divine appointment," she said.

As they finished eating, Morgan said they should soon leave to take the bread to Mark's, and Eric said he should be going. Joyce got him a New Testament and wrote his name in it. Again, his eyes filled with tears. As he and Joyce walked outside together, she shared several Bible verses with him. Eric began to pour out a tale of heartbreak.

"Are you going with me?" Morgan asked Joyce. Eric again said he was leaving. Joyce gave Morgan her special "divine appointment" look and said she really ought to stay with Grandma.

Eric and Joyce walked Morgan to the truck and Morgan showed Eric the bread and pulled away, leaving the two of them alone.

Joyce told Eric to open the New Testament to Matthew 7:7. Together they read, *"Ask and it shall be given you"* and Joyce prayed that God would give Eric a clear understanding of His Word. As they stood in the driveway, Joyce pointed Eric to the verses about salvation in the back of the testament and Eric prayed, confessing his sins and receiving Jesus into his heart.

After Eric had gone, Joyce called Morgan on his cell phone.

"Honey, where are you?" she asked.

"I'm just north of Harrisburg," he answered.

"Eric just received Jesus into his heart," Joyce said.

"Well, that doesn't surprise me," Morgan replied.

"I'll always remember the day I made the Blueberry Buckle," Joyce says. "Praise the Lord!"

Part V

Joyce and Morgan had gone with a retirees' group to the World War II Memorial in Washington, D.C. They enjoyed the trip and the knowledgeable tour guide who filled their driving time with historical trivia.

But the most unforgettable moments for Joyce were at the wall of the Memorial, looking at the 4000 gold stars, each representing 100 men and women who lost their lives for their country.

"I stood there and cried and hoped they would all be in heaven," she said. "It was so touching! I just couldn't stop crying."

A lady walked up and put her arm around her and asked if she had lost a loved one. Joyce nodded, unable to answer, knowing that they were all loved ones to someone.

Then she looked around at the veterans—most in their 80's.

She talked to a man from Littleton, Colorado, whose daughter had brought him to Washington. He said he was a prisoner of war and most of his buddies had been killed. He was wearing his badges. He said that before he died he wanted to see the Memorial.

Joyce shook his hand and thanked him for what he had done for his country.

She talked to some men who were sitting on benches.

"I don't know why I came home and my buddies didn't," one said.

"I believe God had a plan for your life," Joyce responded.

She asked several men about their children, grandchildren and great-grandchildren and told them they were part of God's plan for their lives.

"Someday you will go to another home—your eternal home," she told one man. "Are you ready for that home?"

She gave out the New Testaments she had taken along and told several that the only way they could go to heaven was to ask forgiveness for their sins and invite Jesus to come into their lives.

"I wish I could have been there longer," Joyce reflected. "God knows who those old men are. Was it part of His great plan to send me there? Were they divine appointments?"

CHAPTER TWENTY-SIX

HEARTACHES AND FRAILTIES

Ants in Miyuki's peanut butter, Seth tanning deer hides in the back yard, remembering to turn the egg for Abby's science project, loading the truck with day-old bread for the emus on Mark's farm, selling puppies—there's never a dull moment at The Lighthouse.

Abby had returned to Africa and left her hamster, Teddy Bear, in Morgan's care. One morning, Joyce discovered that the hamster was missing from the glass aquarium on the first floor. Quickly, she summoned Morgan and a student who was living on the third floor to search for him. While they were looking, Miyuki came running downstairs, calling for Morgan. He followed her up the steps and found Teddy Bear tearing up the carpet in the corner of Miyuki's room to build a nest.

At the time of the incident, a mother and her three young children were living in the basement. It was soon discovered that one of the children had removed the screen from the top of the aquarium.

Among the happy moments and humorous happenings at The Lighthouse, there are heartaches and human frailties. One of Joyce and Morgan's greatest concerns is that people will see them as super beings who have no struggles. They have their share.

Multiple Sclerosis

Joyce was diagnosed with multiple sclerosis in 1984. She remembers attending the York Fair in a wheelchair in 1985. Just when it seemed that the ministry might have to come to an end, God touched her body with healing. There have been two reoccurrences and there are occasional reminders that it's still there, but it remains in remission. Recently, a doctor reminded her of that, adding that she should go on doing what she's been doing because it's working.

"I really don't have time to think about it," she says. "If I thought about every little ache and pain, I'd never get anything done." Meanwhile, she travels the three flights of steps inside the house many times daily, often with a full basket of laundry, and continues with a schedule outside the home that defies illness.

Cancer, Deaths, Depression

Shortly after retirement, Morgan received a

diagnosis of colon cancer. When the deaths of Samuel, Joyce's parents, Morgan's father and Annie followed in close succession, he fell into a deep depression.

"He became a man I didn't know," Joyce says sadly. "He'd walk through the house nonstop, wringing his hands."

Much prayer and two surgeries eventually took care of the cancer; prayer plus medication healed the depression.

Separation

Being separated from family is difficult. Amy's abduction was a grim reminder of the distance between them, and it becomes harder for Joyce and Morgan to say goodbye each time she and her family return to Africa. They are very aware that, in the years between visits, they are missing events in Abby, Kari and Peter's lives that can never be recaptured.

Joyce remembers kissing Peter at one such juncture. He reached up and rubbed his cheek, then said, "I'm not wiping off your kiss, Grandma. I'm wiping it in."

Mundane Frustrations

In addition to the obvious heartaches, there are daily frustrations inside The Lighthouse—some as mundane as finding the washer and dryer full of someone else's clothes or sharing the kitchen.

Because it is their responsibility to help out, residents usually clean up after the evening meal. One evening, however, Joyce was gone over the dinner hour and came home to find a sink full of dirty dishes. Tired from her day's activities, she gave in to discouragement and resentment.

"I'll just leave this mess and they can clean it up in the morning," she reasoned.

She went to bed, but couldn't sleep.

"The Lord dealt with me about my attitude," she said, "and I got up and did the dishes. I didn't want them to give me an opportunity for a bad attitude in the morning."

"One thing I have learned is that discouragement is from the enemy," she added. "It happens to me when I get tired. I have to ask myself whether these difficulties will drive me to discouragement or to God."

Misunderstandings

Cultural differences lead to misunderstandings, privacy is nonexistent, items disappear, and people disappoint.

Regarding possessions, Joyce says, "It's important for me to take good care of them because they are God's, so if someone steals from me they are stealing from Him."

"After Uncle Claude died," she continued, "I looked through the dining room cupboards and it was as if the Lord said, 'These things are mine, not yours. Anytime you begin to think they're yours, I'll take them away.'"

In all the years of having people at The Lighthouse, God hasn't taken the things away and neither have the guests. One of the rare disappearances was a vacuum cleaner that was missing after a resident was asked to find another place to live.

Conflicts

Relationships often present challenges. Sometimes there are conflicts between guests and occasionally between a guest and Joyce and/or Morgan.

"The only way I can operate in this house is to confront problems," Joyce says. "Over the years, I've learned that people from other cultures must save face and are often offended by confrontation."

Recently, one guest left The Lighthouse under less than ideal circumstances. When his new housing didn't work out, he called Joyce and Morgan and they welcomed him back. After they all prayed together, they discussed his situation and Joyce and Morgan helped to set him up in an apartment.

Time and Space

Finding time and a place to be alone is always challenging. Sometimes Joyce can be found having her quiet time in a greenhouse attached to the back of the house or on a small balcony adjacent to her upstairs office. Morgan has equipped the greenhouse with fans and a heater so that it's comfortable throughout the year. Joyce has named it "Angel Wings."

Family

"We have always tried to stay close to family, but our lifestyle does cut into my time with my brothers and sisters," Joyce admits. "That's been a sacrifice."

"If I could sum it all up in one word," she wrote recently, "it would be sacrifice. It takes a lot of sacrifice when you are working with people. Your time, your emotions, your family, your earthly belongings, your everything!"

"But, then," she adds, "look what Jesus sacrificed for me. He gave Himself. He died for me. So what we have to do is a drop in the bucket compared to what He did for us."

There are no pretences at The Lighthouse.

"Morgan and I are who we are," Joyce concludes. "We do not pretend to be somebody else. People in our home see us before our first cup of coffee. They see us at our best and at our worst."

"If I'm genuine," she adds philosophically, "I don't have to worry about covering up anything."

She talks about the words "bitter" and "better."

"If I allow trials and frustrations to defeat me, I'll become bitter," she says. "If I give them to Jesus, I get better."

CHAPTER TWENTY-SEVEN

THE LIGHTHOUSE— A STEPPING STONE

"I don't want this to just be about us," Joyce said emphatically as we considered what was written. "Who'd want to read a book about us? We're just an ordinary family."

The Norm

Joyce and Morgan are convinced that what they do is the norm for Christians. "When you're walking with the Lord, the supernatural is natural," Joyce says convincingly. "These things happen every day."

Prayer

When eating at a restaurant, Joyce always asks the server his (or her) name. When the food, is brought, she explains that it is their practice to pray before they eat. "Is there anything we can pray about for you?" she inquires.

Almost always, the server expresses appreciation and gives a request. Joyce tries to make one more contact to give a New Testament when she leaves.

Witnessing

"Witnessing is like going through an apple orchard," Joyce says. "There is ripe fruit and green fruit. When you go through the orchard, you have to pray that the Lord will show you the ripe fruit because if you try to pick the green fruit, you bruise it."

Quiet Time

Morgan and Joyce agree that an essential ingredient of each day is their quiet time with the Lord—preferably in the early morning, and if possible, together.

"The devotional book that means the most to me is Oswald Chambers' *My Utmost for His Highest*," Joyce declares. "Inevitably something from each day's reading meets a need I have that day. If I don't get any other reading done, that and the devotional booklet *Our Daily Bread* carry me through."

Journaling

How someone with such a busy life can keep a journal is a mystery to many. Being without her journals is inconceivable to Joyce.

She holds one in her hand.

"Our lives are so busy. No two days are alike. I wouldn't remember most of this if I hadn't written it down. I don't even know how I had time to do that, but

I did. Obviously, God knew I would need this thing."

Although most of the resident's physical and spiritual birthdays are recorded in one of her many devotional books, she seldom needs the reminder—for they are permanently etched in her mind.

Sample Journal Entries—1987

For my thoughts are not your thoughts, neither are my ways your ways, saith the Lord (Isaiah 55:8 KJV).

Father, my instincts aren't always right. Enable me to know when I should do the opposite of what I feel like doing. Amen.

Going out and doing something for someone else may be the exact opposite of what I feel like doing. But it is often the exact solution to my problem, steering me into a better mood and better attitude. PTL

Praise is saying "yes" to God.
It's an expression of hope.
Sometimes I say, Okay, Lord, show me something hopeful in this!
He always does.
The lovely thing is when I do that, I automatically praise God because He is the source of hope.

Confrontation
It was the week after Mother's Day. Joyce and

Morgan had been out and came home to find an e-mail from a man who had once lived with them. He told her that twenty-six years earlier, she had said something that hurt him, even though he knew it was true. Morgan had asked him to help clean the pool and he had refused. Joyce had told him he was selfish and lazy.

"Today," the man said, "I told my 20-year-old son he is selfish and lazy, and I was reminded of that incident and wept. I want to wish you a Happy Mother's Day and tell you I love you and thank you for putting up with me."

Moving

Most people who come to The Lighthouse have few possessions, so moving in and out usually runs smoothly. It's the moving within the house that makes life interesting.

"We never move (from this address)," Joyce says, "but we move constantly within our home."

What is an office one day may be a bedroom the next. One side of a family room might suddenly hold a cot and an air mattress. A male student's room is quickly transformed into a frilly, girl room when granddaughters come to visit. (The male moves to the cot for that period of time.) "Uncle Claude's" room, the largest bedroom in the house, is now Grandma's room.

On one occasion, a female student needed immediate temporary housing. She had to bring luggage and a fair amount of household goods. A friend brought her to The Lighthouse and Joyce showed her which room she would occupy. It would be a tight fit.

She was to come later in the day. Morgan and Joyce were going out, so they gave her a key to the house. When they returned, she had not arrived. Eventually, they went to bed.

The next morning Joyce went about her usual routine, puzzled about why the girl had not come. Finally, she opened the door to the room to discover her sleeping in the bed, almost hidden by boxes and bags. When the girl was awake enough to answer Joyce's questions, she told her that six of her friends had moved her in after midnight, all of them going up and down the stairs past Joyce and Morgan's bedroom.

Trust

Morgan is often sought out when people need counsel. He has time for all—from the youngest child to the senior citizen. His listening ear draws out hurts, and his wise words give encouragement. Of all the advice he might give, one piece stands out. It's something the Lord taught him through Amy's abduction. He rarely says it without tears.

"It's a lesson I had to learn," he'll tell a seeker. "When I cried out to the Lord about Amy, He answered, 'I know you love Me, but do you trust Me.'"

Stepping Stone

Joyce and Morgan see The Lighthouse as a stepping stone for people who need help getting from one stage of their lives to another.

Some of them have stepped out of addictions, others away from dysfunctional families or broken relationships. Many have stepped into a new culture, often to pursue education. Sandip stepped into the medical profession; Jonas stepped into marriage; Annie stepped into eternity.

Whatever their reason for coming, all have been offered faith. It's been lived out in front of them; it is spoken when they sit in the house (Deuteronomy 6:7). And, at some point, it is clearly presented for them to accept or reject.

Many have invited Christ into their lives during their stay at The Lighthouse. Some have not. Many have continued to walk with the Lord. Some have not. They all received equal treatment.

"Jesus is the Light of The Lighthouse," Joyce explains. "Morgan and I are just the lower lights on the rocks, and we pray that our guests will become beacons, letting their lights shine for Him."

Tribute

"This book wouldn't be complete without a tribute to my mother," Joyce said after having read the manuscript. "I am who I am today because of her. There were no strangers in my mother's life. We were taught there was always room for one more. You just put another plate on the table."

Morgan recalls Joyce's mother with fondness, verbalizing the impact she had on his life.

"She always saw good in people," he says. "A criminal could come to the door and she'd see something good in him."

"Jesus was so evident in my mother's life," Joyce adds. "Her love for Jesus was just so pure and simple. And the wonderful thing is that I see her qualities in my children and grandchildren and in each of my brothers and sisters."

The Big Picture

Seldom do Joyce and Morgan take time to look at the big picture. They've had to in the writing of this book.

"We've been so busy that I never look back," Joyce says. "Now when I do, I'm amazed. I see the majesty of God. This ministry is only possible because Morgan and I have the same goals and are marching to the same drummer. We focus on one day at a time. Each day is the day the Lord has made, and we give Him all the praise for what He does with it."

WITH GRATITUDE

S hortly after the first book about The Lighthouse was published, Joyce began to teach the Bible study at a limited-income apartment building. One Sunday she received a call from Margaret, one of the members of the group, asking if she and Morgan would stop by later in the day.

When they arrived, Margaret pointed Morgan to a dresser drawer and instructed him to bring out its contents. Morgan returned with his hands full of money. Margaret explained that she had earned the money at flea markets and yard sales selling her hand crafts.

"I read your book," she said. "I hope you will write another one. I'm giving you this money for it. I only hope I'm alive to read it."

Margaret didn't live to read this book, but she made it possible. When we sat down to examine our options for its publication and added up the figures, the total was within a few dollars of her gift.

Thank you, Margaret!

Printed in the United States
45198LVS00001B/1-150